BORDER HIGHWAYS

The Story of the Roads and Early Transport in the Scottish Borders

John James Mackay

First published September 1998

Reprinted with minor ammendments February 1999

ISBN 0 9508532 1 6

Published by John James Mackay, 9 Forestfield, Kelso, Roxburghshire TD5 7BX.

Printed by Kelso Graphics, The Knowes, Kelso, Roxburghshire TD5 7BH.

Contents

Foreword

By His Grace the Duke of Buccleuch, KT

On first glance at this book one wonders why no one has made a serious attempt to tackle this fascinating subject before now. On reading it, however, one does realise why. An enormous amount of time-consuming historical research has gone into it and the painstakingly skilful blending of past with present must have presented a challenge that only a most determined author could face.

Although we live in an age where much is taken for granted, roads, and their continuing development, play a major part in the lives of everyone. Parts of this book will have a special fascination for those who identify with particular areas. Older age groups will enjoy reminders of the past. How well do I recall the days of having to drive through a ford on the outskirts of Melrose coming from St. Boswells. Younger people will be able to look back at this book 50 years hence with astonishment at the changes in the 21st century.

All will be united in applauding the author for introducing us in such an enjoyable fashion to an aspect of our heritage trail that winds from Roman days right through to the future.

Buccleuch.

Bowhill, Selkirk.

Introduction

I have divided the book into two sections:

Part I deals with the evolution of roads in the Scottish Borders from Roman times until the present day and gives an account of the events which led to each development along the way; in particular the passing of the various Turnpike Acts from 1750 onwards that did so much to create today's road system.

It is perhaps significant that since that date each of the north-south major roads running through the area (A1, A7 and A68) has undergone a complete change of route for most of its way, showing only too clearly how necessary such radical alterations were to cope with the new types of traffic being introduced.

The main routes and most of the others from Edinburgh to Border towns have a chapter to themselves, followed by a chapter each on cross-routes in the western, central and eastern parts of the area.

Initially there was a temptation to try to include every Borders road, but I very quickly realised that this would entail the work of many more years than I had left. Minor roads have come and gone over the years and little is recorded about them, so that anything to be said would have to be liberally sprinkled with even more 'probables' and 'possibles' than already appear in the text. So, with a few important exceptions, all the roads in this book have in one way or another been connected with the turnpike system covered in chapter 5.

Part II deals with road passenger transport (essentially carriages, stagecoaches and mailcoaches) until the arrival of the railways in the Borders from 1846 onwards. As the railway came to each town, so did stagecoach services cease, leaving only the private carriages of the wealthy on the roads. They too disappeared quite quickly when the motor-car arrived on the scene early in the 20th century. I have endeavoured to trace every stagecoach and mailcoach service in the area for the half century or so of their colourful existence, but almost inevitably some obscure services are waiting to be rediscovered.

The book is the culmination of about four years' research work in libraries, museums and record offices and poring over old maps in numerous places throughout the Borders as well as in Edinburgh, Berwick and London. I soon realised that a thorough exploration of the area by car (and to a much lesser extent on foot) was essential to get a better understanding and this has been a remarkably agreeable part of the task. A relative newcomer to the Borders, I found small corners of this lovely but little-known area of Scotland which I might never have otherwise discovered – serendipity indeed.

Appendix A gives a list of selected books and other reference items containing material dealing with aspects of the subject-matter quoted in the text. Throughout the book there are numerous references to old maps, usually accompanied by the appropriate date – these are described more fully in Appendix B. Readers outside the Borders areas may be unfamiliar with some of the expressions I have used in the book and to assist them I have also included a short glossary as Appendix C.

Except where otherwise stated, I have produced all the photographs and sketch-maps. The sketch-maps do not pretend to be paragons of accuracy, rather they have been included to show the reader the relationship between the modern road systems and those of the days before turnpikes. It is hoped that their inclusion will ease the understanding of the narrative. In many cases I have included more than one route on each map, for not only does this cut down the number of individual diagrams, but it should make it easier to connect one road with its immediate neighbours. Where relevant they show the pre-1975 county boundaries as these determined the siting of many of the toll-houses. A separate map shows all four such counties plus the small part of Midlothian which was included in the Border Region when the reorganisation took place in 1975.

The different types of road are shown conventionally by symbols which differ from map to map and these are clearly marked in each case. Two symbols are standard throughout, however, and to avoid unnecessary repetition these are not explained on the individual diagrams. These are '▲' used to denote toll-houses and '—·—·—·—' for county boundaries.

I have quoted fairly extensively from the valuable sources of The Statistical Accounts of Scotland. The first of these (referred to as the Old or OSA) was produced in the 1790s and the second (New or NSA) appeared some forty years later in the 1830s. They took the form of a detailed census of each parish of each county in Scotland and dealt with such diverse matters as agriculture, the health, welfare and morals of the population, industries, lots of statistical material, landowners and their estates, local fauna and flora, but most of all from the point of view of this book, occasionally on the state of the roads. These accounts were usually written by the local parish minister and ranged from a few terse comments to pages of detail, sometimes even including long lists of the botanical names of the local flora.

Throughout the book, numerous references are made to the old currency which disappeared in 1970 when decimalisation was introduced. As this was almost thirty years ago, many young people today will have little knowledge of things such as shillings and old pence and some of the older ones may have rather short memories of the subject. For this reason I make no apology for informing those readers who wish to know that there were twenty shillings (s.) in the pound, so that one shilling is equivalent to five pence today. In turn the shilling was divided into twelve pence (d.) making two of these old pence very roughly equal to one of today's pence.

It is extremely difficult to compare accurately the value of things in the 18th and early 19th centuries with those of today, but for practical purposes, it may be assumed that inflation between then and now is in the region of one hundred times. In chapter 19 reference is made to the top weekly wage of a guard on a mailcoach as being 30s. (or £1.50 in today's parlance) – multiplying this by one hundred would give an amount of £150 for his wages by modern standards; much more readily understandable. With some of the costs mentioned, by using this method it will be seen that one fare of £7 7s.quoted for a trip on a coach between Edinburgh and London would become the alarming sum of £735 today, revealing just how rich people had to be in those days to travel this way at all.

Finally, it is perhaps inevitable that errors will appear in a book such as this and the responsibility for these must remain firmly with me. I should be grateful if these could be brought to my attention. Similarly any comments on any aspect of the book will be gratefully received and acknowledged.

John Mackay, Kelso,
May 1998.

Acknowledgements

This book could never have been written without the help and support of many people. I wish to acknowledge my debt to the staff of the following organisations and to take this opportunity of thanking them:

The Edinburgh Room and the Reference Library of the Edinburgh Central Library.

The Map Library of the National Library of Scotland, Edinburgh.

Scottish Record Office, Edinburgh.

Berwick Library (Northumberland County Council).

Curator of Road Transport, Royal Museum of Scotland, Edinburgh.

Royal Commission on the Ancient and Historical Monuments of Scotland, Edinburgh.

Museum of Transport, Kelvin Hall, Glasgow.

The Automobile Association, Basingstoke, Hants.

The Archives and Records Centre of the Post Office, Mount Pleasant, London.

The Archives of The Institute of Civil Engineers, Westminster, London.

The following departments of the Scottish Borders Council (and its predecessor Borders Regional Council), that bore the brunt of my inquisitions and were invariably helpful:

Archive and Local History Centre, St. Mary's Mill, Selkirk.

Branch Libraries at Duns, Galashiels, Hawick, Kelso and Peebles.

Museum Headquarters, Selkirk.

Halliwells House Museum, Selkirk.

Sir Walter Scott's Courtroom, Selkirk.

Roads Department at Council Headquarters, Newtown St. Boswells.

I also have to thank Ordnance Survey, Southampton, for their permission to use material from their publications for inclusion in the maps.

I am greatly indebted to His Grace the Duke of Buccleuch for his agreement to write the foreword. With his manifest interest in road matters, it is entirely appropriate that the Duke should have been asked to open the new bridge (Hunter Bridge) over the Tweed at Kelso on 13th August 1998.

One of the endearing qualities of Border folk is their eagerness to help in every possible way in the preparation of books such as this. People from all walks of life have been able to assist with reminiscences, obscure references and even more obscure maps and it is quite amazing what a wealth of knowledge is there for the asking. By naming them I risk the danger of omission and for that reason alone I hope they will accept these thanks for all their valued help and support.

Finally, on a more personal note, I should like to acknowledge the encouragement and tolerance shown by my wife Jenny who, apart from suffering all the inconveniences of the more anti-social aspects of research, was brave enough to agree to read through my final draft and make a number of positive suggestions for improvement. I dedicate this book to her.

Part I

The Evolution of
Roads in the Scottish Borders

Innerleithen *(from Highways and Byways in The Border, A & J Lang 1914)*

Chapter I

Background to
The Scottish Borders

Someone once said that the Scottish Borders were not in Scotland, nor in England, but were 'somewhere in between'. The entire area is not so much a geographical entity perhaps as a vestige of political manoeuvres in the 11th century when a somewhat arbitrary boundary between the Scots and English was first drawn. This created an area, always loosely described as 'The Borders', consisting of the ancient divisions of Merse (which became Berwickshire), Teviotdale and Liddesdale (combined later as Roxburghshire) and Tweeddale (later divided into the two counties of Selkirkshire and Peeblesshire). To complicate matters, Selkirkshire was also known as Ettrick Forest for many years, the 'forest' in this context referring to a hunting area popular with Scottish kings, rather than today's narrower meaning of the word.

Strictly speaking, Dumfriesshire in the west is also a Scottish border county, but its links have tended to be associated with Kirkcudbright and Wigtown to the west, although a possible exception to this is the area surrounding Langholm which appears to maintain a close affinity with the Borders.

The Border counties were the scene of battles, skirmishes, raids and slaughter which the local people had to suffer (or inflict on their fellow countrymen) for hundreds of years until the Union of the Crowns in 1603. The neighbouring English counties of Cumberland and Northumberland suffered many similar indignities during the same period and often their woes were shared in a form of camaraderie which some people might find difficult to understand today.

As the lands were really no more than a wide corridor for moving armies and raiders, the effect of this was almost complete instability on both sides - villages and settlements were frequently destroyed or pillaged together with the inhabitants, animals and crops. So at times when other parts of Scotland and England were enjoying something like comparative peace and prosperity, Borderers paid the penalty for just being where they were. As if the wars were not enough, another great evil in their midst was the reiver movement which involved organised thieving, often linked with extended family groups and sometimes carried out on a large scale under prominent landowners. These reivers came from both sides of the border and they plundered what they could get; livestock, produce, personal belongings and arms, not only from their traditional enemies in the opposing country, but often too from their own countrymen. Their activities reached a climax in the latter part of the 16th century, just as hostilities between England and Scotland were coming to an end, and it was not until James VI assumed control of the whole nation in 1603 that drastic steps were taken to get rid of this menace once and for all.

During those troubled times, the border area was divided on both sides into areas known as Marches, each under the control of a warden who was all too often a leader of one of the reiver bands. North of the border, the East March covered what is now Berwickshire, Middle March was Roxburghshire and the West March, Dumfriesshire.

The corridor effect lasted for a long time after Union, for progress in the area was very slow to take off and ways of communication were in the main used by outsiders rather than local inhabitants who had little or no need for travel. So it was that for many years roads were relatively unimportant to Borderers. It was only with the great improvements in agricultural practices during the 18th century and the growth of industries towards the end of that century that they were to become of importance in getting goods in and out of the area and enable people to move about on wheels rather than on their own feet or on horseback.

When local government in Scotland was reorganised in 1975, the four counties of Berwickshire, Roxburghshire, Selkirkshire and Peeblesshire were combined into one authority known as Borders Regional Council. To it were added the parishes of Heriot and Stow, formerly part of Midlothian. Strange things then happened to the old counties, for they now re-emerged in the guise of District Councils. Selkirkshire simply disappeared and Ettrick and Lauderdale took its place, this then being enlarged by gobbling up large chunks of the counties of Roxburgh and Berwick as well as Heriot and Stow. Berwickshire survived as a name but lost towns like Lauder and Earlston, whilst Roxburghshire found itself without Melrose, one of its more important historic towns. Peeblesshire reverted to its ancient title of Tweeddale.

In 1996 a further reorganisation of local government was made throughout Scotland which led to the disappearance of the District Councils and a new name for the authority - Scottish Borders Council. This time however the boundary remained unchanged. This is essentially the area I shall be dealing with and although strictly speaking it may not be 'Borders' pure and simple, it does provide a suitable region to encompass in this book.

Map 1 – The Scottish Borders area, showing the boundaries of the Counties before Local Government reorganisation in 1975.

I have not stuck religiously to the geographical area, however, for the book would be incomplete without reference to some of the immediate neighbours that are commonly associated with the Borders: places like Biggar just over the boundary into Lanarkshire in the west, Langholm in Dumfriesshire and Berwick-upon-Tweed, a town that never appears to be quite sure where it is. In the 13th century it was Scotland's largest seaport and although it has been part of England since 1482, it lies further north than most of the towns in the Borders and still retains a Scottish feeling about the place. The name Berwick-upon-Tweed is quite a mouthful and like everyone else, I have contracted it to Berwick unless there is any room for confusion.

Edinburgh, too, figures largely when dealing with roads and transport, for the capital was and is the Mecca for all the main routes in the Borders. Without that strong and indeed overpowering influence, the road system would have evolved quite differently.

The story of the Border roads is derived from a heady mixture of the violent history of the area, the difficulties of the terrain, the remoteness of the local people and the lack of need for communications. It was not until the mid-18th century that a spirit of enlightenment changed almost everything, producing a pattern of towns, villages, farms and roads which are still readily recognisable today.

Some roads in the Borders may have survived the Iron Age, but any evidence to support this has long since disappeared. Many of the roads built by the Romans have also gone but there is sufficient left of them to give an indication of their direction and extent. These roads were used long after the Romans left and often subsequent users have built new surfaces on top, so obliterating the visual remains. Some, like stretches of Dere Street, have survived comparatively unscathed after so many years, usually because its way had fallen out of favour, but others have simply been lost when intensive agriculture began to be practised. This became more pronounced with the introduction of deep-ploughing methods, when a lot of our history was simply ripped out of the soil.

Since Roman times, the Dark Ages have kept their secrets well and it is only from the 12th century onwards that we learn something of how whole armies, bands of monks, merchants, thieves and other travellers made their way about the countryside. Unfortunately, here again, the evidence for much of these early highways lies hidden under today's road system or cultivated land and it is only with discarded sections of track in the hills that archaeologists and historians can piece together the layout of these somewhat primitive channels of communication.

The intention of this book is to show how roads evolved to deal with the increasing demand for better communication from the General Post Office, farmers, merchants and the general public.

As will be seen from the ensuing chapters, with the advent of the turnpikes the growth of roads has been a continuing process since the middle of the 18th century with many improvements still being done to cater for today's traffic flows. Compared with other parts of the country though these are very small, and even on the major through routes of the A1, A7 and A68, the peak flows of traffic in August average less than ten thousand vehicles per day, very small compared with even a modest motorway elsewhere. Away from these trunk roads and the ones which connect the main towns, traffic hold-ups are most likely to be encountered when combine harvesters are moving from one field to the next or a shepherd is filling the road with his flock on their way to new pastures.

Almost without exception, the work of turnpike trustees from the 1750s onwards has meant that each major road in the Borders has perceptibly had its route changed to meet the needs of traffic at that time. This is one of the more intriguing aspects of the history of these roads and is dealt with in detail in the appropriate chapters.

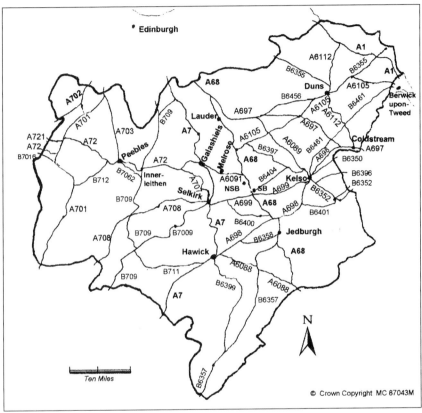

Map 2 – The principal roads of the Scottish Borders.

The Land

Until the agricultural revolution in the 18th century, the road system was very basic and consisted of indifferent through routes from other parts of the country, from which minor tracks spread out to the small towns and scattered communities. Due to the volatile nature of watercourses at that time and the predominance of undrained bog, the roads kept to the higher ground, rarely descending to the floors of valleys unless a river or burn had to be crossed. As bridges were rare, great care had to be taken to find suitable fording places over the network of waterways throughout the area, and often settlements grew up around them.

With tremendous improvements in land drainage from the mid-18th century onwards, most roads built after then could take easier routes by following close to the waterways, so simplifying road construction and avoiding steep gradients. In the days when people walked or went on horseback, gradients were of far less importance, but with the introduction of wheeled traffic such as carriages and carts and the transition to motorised transport in the 20th century, better surfaces and easier grades were becoming essential.

As farming methods improved, so was there a greater need for adequate roads to take the loads to and from the new farms which now dotted the countryside. These roads were often simply improvements to tracks around the fields and even to this day in the Merse of Berwickshire may be found roads which seem to turn left or right at the end of every field. Anyone travelling on the A6112 between Duns and Coldstream by way of Swinton will experience this.

The entire Borders area is essentially of a rural character and of the towns, only Hawick and Galashiels have a population in excess of ten thousand. Today's total population of 103,000 is only 80% of what it was a century ago, most of this change occurring in agricultural districts due to farm mechanisation.

Arable farming, the feature of the prime soils of the Merse of Berwickshire and the fertile valleys of the Tweed and its tributaries, accounts for about 18% of all the land area, whereas almost 64% is grassland (improved or rough), moorland or peat. Woodland accounts for about 16%. Of the small balance, just under one per cent represents developed land, including all the towns, villages, settlements and factory estates throughout the area. Looking down at places such as Hawick and Galashiels from viewpoints on adjoining hillsides, this figure seems unimaginably low, but to get a better impression, take a walk on any of the Cheviot or Tweedsmuir Hills on a clear day - in any direction you will often look in vain for any sight of human habitation.

Rivers and Hills

In a general way, the Scottish Borders area may be regarded as the entire basin of the River Tweed and its many tributaries, notably the Teviot, Ettrick, Yarrow, Leader and Gala Waters. Yet this is not the full story, for the mouth of the river lies entirely within England and there is one tributary, the Bowmont, which runs into England near Kirk Yetholm and then changes its name to Glen before joining the Till and running to the Tweed near Twizel downstream from Coldstream. Just to complicate matters, within the area there are a few small river systems unconnected with the Tweed, the principal ones being the Eye in Berwickshire and the Liddel in the far south of Roxburghshire.

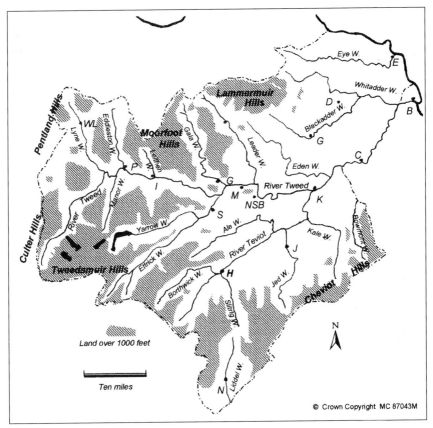

Map 3 – Rivers and Hills.

The area is almost completely surrounded by hill ranges, providing a barrier and a challenge for travellers through the ages. Coming from the north, there is the wide expanse of the Moorfoot and Lammermuir Hills, over which there are two trunk routes from Edinburgh; the A7 and A68, rising to 900 and 1100 feet respectively. The Lammermuirs stretch almost to the North Sea and to avoid them the early main east coast route from Edinburgh had to cross a number of steep gullies, creating other types of difficulties.

To the south-east, the Cheviot Hills are a greater barrier and today there is only one road which crosses the higher parts, the A68 at Carter Bar (1371 feet) on the way into England. In the south, the westward continuation of the Cheviots is crossed by three roads, the B6399 and B6357 (both to Newcastleton) at 1000 and 1250 feet respectively and the A7 to Carlisle which rises to 800 feet at the Dumfriesshire border. The south-west of the area is dominated by the massif of the lonely

19

Tweedsmuir Hills, crossed by three roads, two to Moffat, the A701 rising to 1334 feet and the A708 to 1100 feet and the one to Eskdalemuir (B709) at 1096 feet.

The Culter Hills lie to the west of the Tweedsmuirs with the Tweed forming the boundary between them. No roads go over these hills and those from the west (A702, A72 and B7016) have to pass through the Biggar Gap and the town of the same name. Slightly to the north the A721 from Carluke enters the Borders immediately before the sudden rise of the Pentland Hills.

Nowadays no public roads cross the Pentlands and the Edinburgh-bound A701 and A702 find their way through the gap between these hills and the Moorfoots.

Taken together with the numerous rivers throughout the area, these hill barriers have imposed many problems for road-builders from the Romans onwards.

Chapter 2

The Romans and their Roads

The Roman Occupation of the Borders

Not much is known about the iron-age people who lived in the Scottish Borders before the Roman occupation, but there is ample evidence of a great number of hill-forts in the area. The warlike Selgovae tribe occupied the western part of the area with their 'capital' on the Eildon North Hill. Their more peaceful neighbours, the Votadini, occupied the eastern part and had their main base at Traprain Law in what is now East Lothian. There must have been some means of getting to their sparse tilled fields and hunting grounds and these tracks were probably the first roads - not roads as we know them today, but nonetheless the earliest ways of communication. Wheeled vehicles of a primitive kind were known to them but it is most unlikely that their use would have been very extensive.

The first Roman occupation of the Borders under Julius Agricola in 79AD lasted some twenty years when power was withdrawn as far south as the Tyne-Solway line. In the early 140s southern Scotland was reoccupied by the Romans although by the 160s their installations there were again abandoned. Around 209 the last invasion was made by the emperor Septimus Severus who personally led a large force northwards, but it appears that great difficulties were encountered in achieving reoccupation and when the emperor died in 211, the opportunity was taken to leave Scotland for the last time.

Roman Roads

During these occupations, large camps were built to house their armies, together with forts and fortlets, and a good road system was required to service these. The roads they made were to such a high standard that some of them lasted for a very long time. Even today there are remains of miles of Roman roads clearly in evidence, especially in upland areas. Along these roads poured a stream of vehicles and people, employed in the defence, administration or provisioning of this, the most far-flung part of their entire empire.

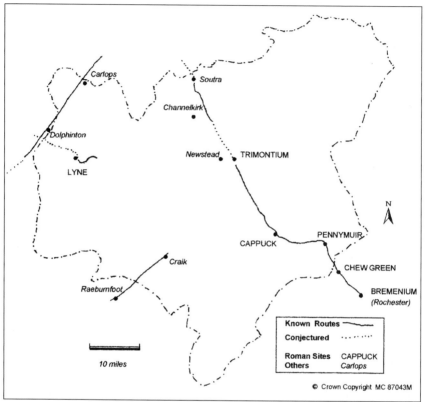

Map 4 – Roman Roads.

The basic road framework, probably conceived and laid down during the first period of occupation, is a simple one. The main artery of the system was the road known to us since Saxon times as Dere Street, running from Corbridge in Northumberland and driven north over the Cheviot Hills by way of Redesdale, across the valleys of the Teviot and Tweed (intentionally or otherwise running more or less in a line between the areas of the two resident tribes), then up the west side of Lauderdale along the ridgeway which separates the valleys of the Allan Water and the Leader. Crossing the Lammermuir Hills to the west of Soutra Hill, parts of the route can still be followed. From there it descended into the Lothian plain then on to the shores of the Forth estuary close to what is now the City of Edinburgh.

Dere Street had to cross both the Teviot and the Tweed; probably a simple matter in the summer months when levels were low, but at other times these would have created major problems. Ferries might have been used, although it is quite likely that bridges of a sort had been built. It has long been considered that there must have been such a bridge near Trimontium and although there are no traces of such a structure above the ground, archaeologists are still searching the area for evidence.

This was the road along which the main thrust of the Roman occupation would have taken place and it led past the major Roman fort of Trimontium near today's village of Newstead, close to the hill-fort 'capital' of the Selgovae on Eildon Hill North. For many years it had been thought that this had been destroyed by the Romans when they first arrived in 79AD, but recent researches have shown that the site was probably already abandoned by that time.

Trimontium (aptly named from the three Eildon peaks) was the hub of the transport system, for here (or nearby) another road is thought to have crossed on a west-east axis. Little is known of the eastern way to the coast at Berwick other than the excavated remains of camps at Maxton, Wooden (near Kelso), Carham, East Learmouth and Norham, all on the south bank of the Tweed. These point to a road having connected them with Trimontium in the west and Tweedmouth in the east where a known Roman road from the south had ended.

Fortunately there remains some evidence of the western arm as it made its way up the valley of the Tweed, through Lanarkshire and across Ayrshire to the Clyde estuary. In the Borders, a short stretch of the road itself exists to the west of Peebles by Jedderfield Farm where it swings uphill to avoid a small burn. Using the fort at Lyne and the temporary camps found along the way at Innerleithen, Eshies (east of Peebles) and Castlecraig at Kirkurd, it may be readily imagined that the Roman road had more or less followed the route of today's A72 on the north side of the Tweed, then the valleys of the Lyne and Tarth Waters into Lanarkshire. However tempting this may be, it is known that in recent geological times the Tweed has changed its course along its valley on a number of occasions and in any case it is quite likely that the entire area by the river was one vast marsh. Under these circumstances, the road-builders would have had to make deviations away from areas where tributaries ran into the main river, just as has been found at Jedderfield.

Between Innerleithen and Trimontium the position becomes even more difficult, with the only Roman evidence found so far being the remains of a stone structure at Easter Langlee east of Galashiels. Like the other evidence, it lies to the north of the Tweed and from this it could be reasonably assumed that most of the road lay on that side. Of course it had to cross the river somewhere to reach Trimontium on the other bank and this could have been achieved by a ford or a bridge, the most favourable site for this probably being in the neighbourhood of Lowood where in medieval times a bridge had been built. Alternatively, the road could have continued eastwards to meet Dere Street on the north side of the Tweed.

Even less is known of another route which led from the Tweed southwestwards by the Ettrick valley, then following the Moffat Water to the valley of the Annan near Beattock, where it joined the western road from the Carlisle area northwards to the Clyde valley.

Evidence of another Roman road in the Borders was not excavated until 1946 when a section was uncovered in what is now the Craik Forest, west of Hawick and close to the Dumfriesshire boundary. It is now known that it followed the Teviot and Borthwick Waters across Craik Cross Hill to Raeburnfoot just north of Eskdalemuir village.

Finally, a Roman road connecting Annandale and the valley of the Forth passed through the far northwest of the Borders for a distance of six miles. It entered Peeblesshire from Lanarkshire near Dolphinton, made its way to the west of West Linton and through Carlops where it crossed into Midlothian. Much of this road has been lost, mainly because a medieval road was built over much of it, although stretches have perished from extensive farming activity in the more fertile areas.

Road Construction

With the exception of the stretch of Dere Street between Ulston Moor and Lilliardsedge in Roxburghshire, these roads were not '*straight as a rule before him lay, for many a mile the Roman way*'. Unlike the southern half of Britain, the terrain of Northumberland and much of Scotland made it difficult even for the Romans to construct roads in their customary manner, but where long straight stretches were not possible, they did preserve this concept by building up the actual line in short straight sections. The work was probably mostly done by skilled military personnel using crude but effective instruments for sighting and measuring angles and heights, the likes of which would not be seen again for seventeen hundred years.

The average overall width of the Roman roads was about 20 feet, although sometimes such as on parts of Dere Street over Ulston Moor, this could be as much as 30 feet. The basic dimensions of the highway would have been dictated by the width of the wheels on their chariots and carts, and by a curious coincidence this appears to have been very close to the standard gauge of British railway lines of four feet eight and a half inches. Evidence of this was found on wheel-tracks at a fort on Hadrian's Wall at Housesteads in Northumberland and also at Ardoch in Perthshire. It is not known whether this standard was a Roman introduction or had been used by the indigenous tribes for their primitive vehicles, but such vehicles formed a sufficiently high proportion of those in use to make their presence a modifying constraint on the design and construction of the road system. Men and their animals only made a relatively small contribution to the wear and tear of a road, but unsprung vehicles, equipped with metal tyres and heavily laden, would have dug into any ordinary running surface - and more so on gradients. Armed with these factors, it can be seen how skilled the Romans were in their design and construction of the road system in the undulating countryside of the Borders by reinforcing them on gradients.

The surfaces of these roads were metalled with material such as cobbles and grit or rammed gravel, normally showing a camber, with the crown of the road stiffened by a mid-rib, and all held together by heavy kerbing. Surface water was collected in ditches, but on sloping ground, culverts were provided to carry excess water under the road and away to the downward side of the slope. The choice of foundations for the road was determined by the circumstances locally; for example at a point northeast of Dolphinton at Ingraston, there was an area of peat-bog and here the road was laid on a thin layer of gravel and sand as heavier stones would have been insupportable.

When the Romans built their road over Craik Moor, they found that the basic rock was overlaid with fragmentary rocks and pockets of peat, neither of which was very desirable for road-building. The Romans overcame these by digging them away to expose the sound rock, then cambering that to produce a wide thoroughfare complete with side-ditches. In the neighbourhood of Soutra in the Lammermuir Hills, part of the road was carried on a projecting terrace, extending out from the slope of the hill by as much as 50 feet. These works were undoubtedly the forerunners of the modern civil engineering equivalents of cuttings and embankments.

Chapter 3

Pre-Turnpike Roads

The Anglo-Saxon Invaders

When the Romans finally left, a curtain seemed to fall over the country to create the Dark Ages and little is known about events which took place until the Anglo-Saxon invasions in the 6th century, leading to the eventual occupation of the Borders area by them. The warring Selgovae probably continued to fight with their neighbours, but to what extent their lives had changed with the Roman occupation is speculative. They would have made some use of the Roman road system, just as those after them did for well over a thousand years.

Under the Northumbrian kings, Anglo-Saxon power exerted a strong influence on the countryside extending as far as the present day site of Edinburgh. The Celts never had towns nor even villages as we know them now, but it was not long before the invaders had introduced these forms of settlement, albeit it a very modest way, by creating primitive communities in places such as the valley of the Bowmont Water in the Cheviots. Here, settlements at Morebattle, Yetholm, Whitton, Clifton, Sourhope, Shotten and Halterburn, all recognisable today, were included in a grant of property to the monks of Lindisfarne by the Northumbrian king, done by appropriating land from the remnant population, descendants of the iron age folk. They would have had to move to make way for the conquerors or have become totally assimilated by them.

In time settlements grew up in other valleys of the Cheviots and in the Lammermuir Hills, using sites which avoided the extremes of high ground and the maze of marshes of the lower river valleys - preferably on well-drained areas on river gravel or light glacial soils. We may therefore assume that some of the first district roads followed contours on the upper sides of these valleys to connect the communities, avoiding the marshy low-lying areas. Rudimentary bridges might have been constructed about this time, but it is doubtful whether these ever crossed the wider rivers, at least at that stage.

Only later did they start to form settlements lower down, leading to the formation of hamlets, villages and small towns, many of the sites of which still exist. There would have been an improvement in the structure of the roads connecting these places, for without doubt goods had to be transported from place to place and it was very likely that sledges or even some form of primitive carts might have been drawn by animals. These required something more than narrow tracks sufficient for the passage of a man and his horse, but of course nothing like the standard achieved by the earlier Romans.

It was in the 11th century that for the first time a boundary was roughly established between Scotland and England and a little later that parishes began to appear as a feature of church and local administration. Many of the parish boundaries date from that time.

Dere Street

As will be seen below, Dere Street continued to be the main highway serving most of the central area of the Borders for those travellers proceeding north- or southwards. Indeed it would do so until its usefulness came to an end in the latter half of the 18th century when it was replaced by roads capable to of taking wheeled traffic, since when it has continued to be used by hill farmers, walkers and riders of all kinds. It has had many names in its time, perhaps the most curious being the title of 'Watling Street' which persisted until well into this century. This arose from a misunderstanding and confusion with the actual Watling Street, a Roman road which ran from Dover to Chester - nowhere near the Borders. This title appeared on the first large-scale Ordnance Survey maps and not content with that, against the road was also shown (for good measure) *Via Militaris Antoninus Iter 5th*, roughly translated as 'The military road of Antonine's fifth journey'.

For parts of its length, Dere Street was used as a division between parishes, signifying the continuing importance of the Roman road, not only as a highway but also as a meaningful landmark. In Roxburghshire for example, at Lilliardsedge south of St. Boswells, it separated the parishes of Ancrum and Maxton and further to the south-east, the parishes of Oxnam and Hownam.

Roads serving the Great Abbeys

The next set of conquerors were the Normans; not an invasion of usurping people this time, but a ruling élite, imposing new patterns on the existing rural population. Norman lords carved out estates for themselves and monastery settlements were established on old Anglo-Saxon sites; Coldingham in 1089, Melrose in 1130 and Jedburgh in 1118. New establishments were set up at Kelso, Dryburgh and Abbey St. Bathans, largely under the influence of King David I. These monasteries (and the magnificent abbeys which went with most of them) were the first substantial buildings in the Borders and they made a large impact on the local economy with the growing trade in locally-produced wool as well as grain; much of which was exported through the port of Berwick, at that time still a Scottish town.

The prosperity of the Border monasteries continued to grow and the demand for more wool, particularly from Flanders and as far away as Italy, led to the monks acquiring lands outside the Borders area which were then farmed as granges. Kelso Abbey had such outlying properties in places like Lesmahagow in Lanarkshire and Kilwinning in Ayrshire as well as nearer home in Dumfriesshire and Midlothian. From such places the raw or semi-processed wool would first have gone to the appropriate monastery before finally being taken to Berwick, where by the 13th century there were at least fifteen warehouses owned by religious houses. Some form of track-way would have been needed and this would have given rise to the first positive attempts since Roman times to create a road system. If everything had been carried by pack-horses, then the way need not have been very sophisticated, but it is quite likely that even from the early days animal-drawn carts of a sort had been used, necessitating some kind of hard causeway to prevent loads getting bogged down in poor weather. Certainly by 1300 carts were in use, for it is recorded that husbandmen (farmers) at Redden, one of the granges not far from Kelso Abbey, had to go to Berwick weekly, summer and winter, with one-horse carts carrying corn and returning with loads of salt and coal.

It is unfortunate that no traces of these monastery roads have ever been found, although it could well be that some of them lie under today's road systems.

At the same time, roads of a sort were needed to connect the Border monasteries with the new capital at Edinburgh, moved there from Dunfermline by Malcolm Canmore in the 11th century. Edinburgh was beginning to exert an influence on the rest of the country - even to the somewhat isolated Borders country.

It was this need for communication with the capital that gave rise to a north-south system of early roads; serving monastery, castle and administration. Soon afterwards, they were also used by armies from both sides of the border which were to ravage the area for hundreds of years before peace finally came with the union of the crowns in 1603.

The road north from Jedburgh Abbey was thought to have passed through Ancrum and Melrose before crossing the Tweed near Darnick either by a ford or a primitive bridge. From there it went over the moors to Blainslie and Lauder to join Dere Street through Oxton, Channelkirk, Soutra and on to Dalkeith and Edinburgh. This way endured for a very long time.

The road from Kelso would have served both the abbey and the castle as well as the thriving town at Roxburgh. By 1330 a bridge had been built across the Tweed near Roxburgh to connect with Wester Kelso on the east bank, but all trace of this has long since gone. Originally the way may have made directly for Dere Street but later we do know that it followed a route, parts of which still exist today, past

Smailholm then almost straight to Legerwood, close by Boon, passing east of Lauder and making for Oxton where it joined the road from Jedburgh.

There is no reference to a separate road from Dryburgh Abbey and if there had been one, all evidence of it has disappeared.

It would be realistic to expect that Melrose monks might have shared the same road to Edinburgh as those from Jedburgh, but another way appears to have been in use, known as The Girthgate. Like the others, it was probably no more than a footpath at best and the actual route it took has been the subject of much debate over the years. It is thought that girth meant sanctuary and could have referred to such places as Soutra, Stow or Melrose. Nowhere is it mentioned prior to 1743 when it was described by Milne, the Melrose historian, who said it ran from a bridge at Bridgend to Soutra. Some people think that it may not have existed at all as a separate way but merely a misunderstanding regarding the already-established way from Jedburgh to which reference has already been made. It was not shown on Roy's Military Map of 1750 (usually accepted as reliable) but does appear in the 1771 Berwickshire map by Armstrong, running about two miles west of Dere Street, the two ways coming together just to the south of Soutra. The latest edition of the Ordnance Survey Pathfinder 1:25000 series shows 'Girthgate' in at least three places alongside a footpath, presumably on the evidence of the Armstrong map.

There had been a road of sorts between the monastery at Coldingham and the small settlement of Dunbar on the coast further north, so there may have been no need for a southern connection, especially as the terrain between Coldingham and Berwick would have been very wild at that time.

These roads obeyed the same unwritten rules as the earliest ones in Anglo-Saxon days; they kept to the drier ground above the boggy river valleys, descending to them only to cross streams and rivers. Perhaps too most were little used in the winter months or when the weather was poor. Fortunately for the wool industry based on the monasteries, most of the work connected with it would have been done in the summer months, so it was possible to move the loads to the coast in the best available conditions.

The monasteries were to suffer terrible blows, the first being in 1482 when Berwick was lost to the English for the final time, so depriving the monks of this valuable outlet for their wool exports. Then in 1543, Henry VIII saw a solution to the constant problem of his northern neighbour - the marriage of his five year old son Edward to the infant Mary, daughter of King James V of Scotland - *'Let the children be betrothed and later married and England and Scotland would be eventually under one ruler'*. The lack of enthusiasm from the Scots led Henry to adopt what came to be called 'the rough wooing'; a little force being seen as a way to achieving his ambition. To this end the Earl of Hertford (later to become the Duke of Somerset) was given a free hand to wreak havoc in southern Scotland. For almost five years there was a relentless barrage of attacks on the Borders and further north at Edinburgh and the Lothians. It was only with the death of Henry in 1547 that the pressure eased; within two years the war came to an end with armies being withdrawn and assurances given that attacks on Scotland were to cease.

During these ferocious years, all the Border abbeys and the associated monastic buildings had been destroyed or severely damaged; virtually every town, village, settlement and fortification flattened, and the people left without animals or shelter.

Whilst all this had been going on, the Border reivers were becoming much more adventurous, taking advantage of the chaotic conditions to further their own ends by virtually any means. They operated from both sides of the border with equal disregard for any form of authority, making for even more unstable conditions for the long-suffering innocent members of the population. It was not until James VI became the monarch of both countries in 1603 that sufficient pressure was exerted to bring their activities to a halt.

When the Reformation came to Scotland, the wrecking of monasteries which had been all too familiar in England did not occur north of the border. It would have been unnecessary anyway (Henry had seen to that) and what was left of them was merely allowed to fall into even further decay so that the few remaining monks did not remain for any length of time. Here was a small corner of Scotland, still relatively remote from the capital by the barrier of the Pentlands, Moorfoots and Lammermuirs, left reeling from centuries of depredation by armies and reivers alike and the loss of employment with the departure of the old monastic orders. The need for roads to the outlying granges simply disappeared and it would not have been long before the tracks of them went as well. The people of the Borders now had to rely on their own farming methods, primitive as they were, merely to survive. They had little need of a road system at all.

Military Movements

Armies had to carry heavy loads of supplies including cannon, a daunting task for man and beast, especially over the wild ranges of hills such as the Cheviots and Lammermuirs. This alone was a very good reason for not resorting to winter expeditions. There was an alternative route nearer the east coast, but here the roads were even worse than the inland ones and more dangerous, for deep ravines had to be negotiated at places such as the Dunglass and Pease Burns. There had been a stone bridge at Dunglass since early times (and it is still there) but the access to it was treacherous. The Pease was even trickier, as the only possible way to cross it was by steep inclines to a ford close to the seashore at its mouth. In Bleau's Atlas of 1649 a bridge was shown, but this may have been only a temporary affair as all trace of it has vanished.

This way was, however, used by at least four English armies: Edward I on his way to Dunbar Castle, the Earl of Hertford on his return from the sacking of Edinburgh in 1544, the next expedition of 1547 which led to the battle of Pinkie and, a century later, Cromwell's troops in the invasion of 1650. The routes commonly used for these forces often depended upon which side had control over the strategic Border fortresses of Roxburgh, Hume and Berwick. The invasions of England by Scottish troops, however, all seemed to have followed the Soutra route, although in 1496 a curious way by Haddington and Cranshaws was taken.

Soutra then was the favoured way, with the bonus of a hospice for the tired, sick and wounded at one of the highest points on the road. Dere Street, very much an important part of Border communication, carried these armies when they entered Scotland from Redesdale, but other ways into the country had to be found when they came from further west. From Carlisle and the northwest of England, the obvious route was up Liddesdale and a 12th century charter does refer to a road to Roxburgh taking this way. Unfortunately there is no other reference to it since then, but it might have been a road the remains of which have been found about one mile east of the B6357 (Newcastleton to Jedburgh) in the Saughtree area. Much more is known about the way further north.

Wheel Causeway

North of Saughtree, branches joined the road from the valley of the North Tyne. As it proceeded north-eastwards, it divided more than once, but all the evidence indicates that most of these branches ultimately made their way by Southdean or Chesters to Jedburgh. The road (or roads) became known as the Wheel Causeway or Causey, a title which first appeared in the 16th century in the Letters and Papers of Henry VIII as *'the While or Wheele Caussye'* where it was included as one of the *'ingates and passages forth of Scotland'*. Other early references appear to indicate that the name may have been an actual place rather than a road: in 1533 *'they entered Scotland at Whele Causey'* and in 1585 *'.....crossed the border at the Whele Causey a mile within Scotland'*. The name has nothing to do with wheels and appears to have come from a long-gone village and church on the way called Wheel or Le Whele, the site of which now lies deep in Wauchhope Forest some twelve miles south of Jedburgh. An itinerary of Edward I in 1296 refers to a route from Jedburgh to Castleton in Liddesdale by way of Wheel.

For some time this way was thought to have been Roman in origin and in the book by Andrew and John Lang 'Highways and Byways in the Border' written in 1914, reference is made to armies *'going across the hills by the old Roman way of the Whele Causeway into Liddesdale and thence on to Carlisle'*. Even as late as 1961, the half-inch Bartholomew map of Tweeddale showed the Wheel Causeway by name with 'Roman Road' next to it. It is now known that the Romans did not build this particular road.

Alexander Jeffrey in his History and Antiquities of Roxburghshire (1836) makes some scathing points about the damage which had been done to this road:-

> *'It presents the same features..... in places where it has not been destroyed by the farmers converting the stones with which it is paved into fences for sheep walks. We regret to be forced to say that, during the course through the farm of Hyndlee, the work of destruction has been so well done within these few years, as to render it difficult to find a trace of this remarkable work of antiquity. Landlords and farmers do not seem to have the least compunctious feeling in thus dealing with the remains of a byegone age. In their eyes the best constructed Roman Causeway is not equal to an ordinary farm road; and the most sacred relic would, without hesitation, be thrust into the gap of a fauld dyke.'*

East Coast Road

One of the effects of the Union of the Crowns in 1603 was that for the first time land communications had to be established across the border for peaceful purposes. This was not seen immediately, but in time five major highways would wend their ways through the Borders to connect England with the Scottish lowlands and, in particular, with Edinburgh. The best known of these, although not always the most popular, was the East Coast Road from Edinburgh to Berwick through Haddington and Dunbar, crossing into Berwickshire at Dunglass and passing Cockburnspath and Ayton before reaching the English border at Lamberton.

This road is dealt with in detail in Chapter 6 and it is sufficient here to mention that despite the drawbacks of the dangerous ravines and lonely moors on the way, it was always a serious rival with Soutra for the main cross-border traffic. As will be seen, the first stage- and mailcoaches between the two capitals ran this way and in time it acquired the somewhat inflated sobriquet of Great North Road. It was the first road in Scotland to have any form of postal service and a post office was established at Cockburnspath in 1693, long before anywhere else in the Borders. It was necessary to arrange staging-posts for the horse traffic starting to use the road and soon the local people were deriving benefit from the provision of the vital board, lodgings and stabling facilities required on the way, leading to some of the first primitive travellers' inns.

Drove Roads

Drove roads were extensively used for about a hundred and fifty years, starting shortly after the time of the Union of the Parliaments in 1707 and lasting until the middle of the 19th century. Much has been written about the romance of them and in Haldane's book 'The Drove Roads of Scotland' he gives an admirable account of their history.

The demand for beef arose from the dramatic growth of London during this period and the increasing size of the army and navy. With no refrigeration, the most economic way of getting beef to the southern markets was to drive the cattle there at a leisurely pace, ensuring that they had enough to eat on the way. This meant selecting routes that afforded free or cheap grazing on the journey. There was no shortage of such ways through the Borders, for at that time few of the hillsides were being extensively used by local farmers. From all accounts, the drovers were welcomed by most people in the Borders, for not only were they a source of income during their passage, but they also brought news from the outside world.

The beef from the small hardy highland black cattle was much in demand and this breed was the one most commonly seen on their slow way through the area. In the middle of the 18th century it was estimated that the number of cattle entering England from Scotland was 80,000 head per year, more than half of them coming through the Borders. From the Highlands the cattle had been driven towards points or 'trysts' at Crieff and Falkirk prior to the long journeys into England. From Falkirk, there was a choice of ways and each drover would have had his own favourite one. Some of them opted to follow the Clyde and Annan valleys on the west side of the country, whilst others preferred to pass through the Borders. Those in the latter category would, in practice, enter the area on the main drove road over the Pentland Hills at Cauldstane Slap, follow the Lyne Water through West Linton and on to Romanno Bridge and Peebles. Romanno Bridge was the first toll and much of its revenue was derived from driven cattle. Often drovers took circuitous routes to avoid the toll charges, the success or otherwise of these ruses largely depending upon the generosity of local farmers.

From Peebles, there were two main routes onwards, although there were other lesser used ones as well. The first led south over the hills to Craig Douglas on the Yarrow, just to the east of St. Mary's Loch then by Tushielaw into the Ettrick valley. From there it passed by Buccleuch to Deanburnhaugh on Borthwick Water, then into Teviotdale and over the border to Dumfriesshire.

The second one went from Peebles to Traquair then over the Minch Moor road into the Yarrow valley at Philiphaugh, close by Selkirk. From here the drovers had a choice of routes, many of them now lost to us. A number took the way towards

Hawick, but there was a strong disagreement between locals and drovers in 1777 and after that time the town was usually avoided. Thereafter most of the drovers passing through Selkirk elected to go over the Cheviots, crossing the border into England and descending the valleys of the North Tyne and the Coquet using a myriad of tracks through the grasslands.

Few if any of the drove roads had been built as such; rather older tracks had been used and in time had spread sideways with the passage of the black cattle. Sometimes two parallel walls had been built to contain the droves and so avoid disputes with farmers; examples of these can still be seen on the two routes from Peebles, the first just south of the town and the other on Minch Moor above Traquair. As will be shown later, plans had been made at Cauldstane Slap and Minch Moor for the drove roads to be made into turnpikes, but nothing came of either proposal and today these and most of the other drove roads are used only by local farmers and walkers.

Few drovers attempted to go further east, for this meant crossing the rich farmlands of lower Teviotdale and the Merse of Berwickshire, both quite unsuitable for this kind of traffic.

After the end of the Napoleonic wars, the demand for Highland beef quickly fell and with it came the ultimate end of droving. By 1850 it was all over, with most of the old roads simply disappearing into the surrounding grassland.

Other Roads

Apart from the main ways already referred to, all four Border counties had other medieval roads; most of them rediscovered by archaeologists from the 19th century onwards. These discoveries were mainly in the upland areas not yet improved by farmers, for otherwise today's methods (particularly deep-ploughing) would have totally destroyed what evidence had remained. As better roads were built at lower and more manageable levels, so these early ways became disused and as few of them had been metalled in any way, their finding depended upon the fact that many of them showed through the rough moorland surface as green lanes, consisting of a set of hollow tracks worn by the passage of men and animals.

Such trackways were particularly numerous in the areas of Liddesdale, Tweedsmuir and the Cheviot Hills; more than would actually have been necessary for communication purposes and as many of them were referred to as 'Thief Roads' their chief use becomes apparent. These were no ordinary thieves, but the lawless reivers who for hundreds of years until the 17th century had plagued the Border areas on both sides of the national boundary, causing almost as much alarm as the

Coaches on an outing on the road from Berrybush to Tibby Shiels, St. Mary's Loch,
about 1900. This way was probably an early track which later became a drove road.
Now no longer a public road. (Reproduced by courtesy of Scottish Borders Council
Museum Services)

entire armies which passed through. The first reference to this type of road was as
early as 1255 when a Thewesrode was mentioned on the English side of the
Cheviots. An old road from Sourhope to the border was described in 1597 as '*a*
passage and bye-way for the theefe'.

Some of these carried names, for instance in Selkirkshire, the track to St. Mary's
Loch on the Yarrow from Hopehouse on the Ettrick was known as '*Captain's*
Road' and indicated as such in the current editions of the Ordnance Survey. The
captain was probably the title of a member of one of the Border Wardens who had
control over the Marches.

Proceeding south-eastwards from Hownam village to the English border in the Cheviots, 'The Street' is an interesting example. Despite its name, it has no connection with the Romans and there are no early references to it by that name, but must be very old for its way marks part of the boundary between the parishes of Hownam and Morebattle. Like some of the others, along sections of its length it appears to have been widened to take some form of primitive wheeled vehicles, but this was probably done towards the end of its active life at the end of the nineteenth century. It was reported that about that time loads of Scottish oatmeal were still being regularly carted along this way to supply isolated shepherds on the English side of the border.

Ironically perhaps, many of these old tracks survive today only because they were selected to be part of a designated route taken by long-distance footpaths, in particular the Southern Upland Way which runs from the Clyde coast to the North Sea.

Some of the hill tracks have in time been superimposed by modern roads and in such cases, all evidence of the old way has been irretrievably lost. Lower down in the valleys, only tiny fragments of old roads survive, due not only to farming activities but also the effects of watercourses changing their line in times of flooding, effectively washing away the remains. It is quite likely that many of the lowland medieval roads were those which were improved in the 18th century to make the first turnpike roads; a mere look at Roy's Military Map of 1750 reveals a road pattern much of which can today be identified with major routes serving the Borders. In dealing with individual roads in later chapters, references are made to such old remnants as still exist.

It is disappointing that so few of the medieval roads of lowland areas of Roxburghshire and Berwickshire have survived, but these were and remain the richest farming areas in the Borders and what became disused soon disappeared. A map of these areas shows a plethora of roads serving farms and outlying areas - it is quite likely that these follow the ancient ways without many alterations having been made at all, so it could be argued that many of the medieval roads have been preserved, albeit accidentally, insofar as their locations are concerned.

Before leaving these old roads, mention should be made of another type. Over the Lammermuir Hills there were several tracks connecting the small fishing ports of East Lothian with Border towns such as Lauder. These were used by people (often women) carrying heavy fresh loads of fish and inevitably perhaps these tracks became known as 'Herring Roads'. In warm weather it is difficult to imagine just how fresh the fish would have been after the long tramp over the hills.

Chapter 4

The Effects of the Agricultural Revolution

The preparation for agricultural improvement had started in a modest way in the 17th century with a series of acts to encourage the division, consolidation and enclosure of land. At the time, this had little effect in the Borders and in any case, this legislation was not in itself sufficient to permit anything radical, although it did create a framework within which the landowners could operate later on.

Agriculture played such an important part in the growth of Border roads and as the 18th century saw the first real developments which were going to change everything, it is perhaps worthwhile to pause for a look at the Borders at the beginning of that century.

Although essentially a rural community, there were urban settlements; the Royal Burghs of Jedburgh, Peebles, Selkirk and Lauder and those of a lesser status as Burghs of Barony at places such as Duns, Earlston, Galashiels, Hawick, Kelso, Melrose, Eyemouth, Greenlaw and Coldstream. Two important Royal Burghs had been lost in the fifteenth century - Berwick to become the most northerly town in England whilst the destruction of Roxburgh for tactical reasons meant that nothing remains above the surface on its site just across the Tweed from Kelso.

Many of these towns had their own trades and weekly markets but of course nothing was on an extensive scale and it was likely that much of the trading would have been by barter rather than by cash. The little things that were needed from outside each community came on horseback from some distant place to be sold in the small shops of the towns, or packmen came round to the cottages and the lairds' houses with a very limited assortment of goods.

There were few industries but these were quite primitive: a few woollen mills to take advantage of fast water at Hawick and Galashiels, probably for waulking (felting) of locally produced cloth for blankets, etc. In general, the textile industry which was to become such an important part of Border life was still in its infancy and most of it carried out in the home rather than in mills.

In the country, things had not changed very much at all from what had been the case a century before and the scenery was very different from that of today. The flat haughs by the rivers lay largely unused for much of the year due to poor drainage and threatening rivers. In fact drainage was virtually unknown, so that even away from rivers, if the land were at all flat it was often very difficult to handle except during an exceptionally dry spell. Only on the drier and steeper hillsides did ploughing become a practicality, although naturally the soil on such sites tended to be poorer and much more tricky to work with the clumsy teams of oxen and primitive wooden ploughs. The only grain sown was either an inferior grey oat, which at best gave a threefold increase in the seed planted, or bere which although the least nutritious of the barleys, was grown because it was believed to be the only sort that would flourish in the conditions of the time and area.

The houses of the farmers and peasantry were still of sods and wattling and even the laird himself was still enduring the acute discomfort of a cold draughty fortified house or tower which had been built in previous years for defence rather than more peaceful purposes. Many of the workers' hovels were clustered together, not just for convenience, but as a vestige of more troubled days 150 years before when protection was vital. Often they surrounded the house of the tenant farmer, creating a farm 'toun' or town. From them they went out to their run-rigs - strips of land in various fields within the landlord's domain which they shared with others, a cumbersome method which in time led to run-rig being used to describe the old pre-improved style of farming. The farm-land generally was devoid of trees and hedges except for a few clumps round the lairds' houses to provide shelter. Away from the cultivated fields, the unused area was aptly known as waste and at this time, it made up the bulk of all the Borders lands.

With a system so atrocious, with land uncleaned, unlimed, unmanured, undrained and with no provision for crop rotation, it frequently happened that the yield could scarcely feed the inhabitants of the district, leading to starvation when the weather was particularly bad and crops failed. With snow on the moors and only a few days' food left for their cattle, the minister of the remote parish of Ettrick, Thomas Boston, recorded *"The Lord was with us in praying and preaching from Joel 1 18, 'Now do the beasts groan, etc.' The Lord heard our prayers. The morrow was no ill day, but on the Friday the thaw came with a west wind."*

Yet within a century we find a countryside not very different from today's picture, with stone farm buildings and cottages, villages, Georgian mansions, woodland, hedges, drained mosses and reclaimed haughs, improved hill pastures and a reasonable network of roads and bridges: in other words an agricultural revolution had taken place. What factors had brought this about?

There can be little doubt that the catalyst for change was created with the 1707 Act of Union with England. Markets hitherto closed to Scottish produce were now becoming available, not just south of the border but also in the emerging colonies in the Americas, Asia and Africa. England's industrial revolution was just about to start and there was a similar but smaller one in Glasgow and surrounding area. London's growth at this time was staggering and there was a rapid increase in the size of the army and navy to enable Britain to play its part in Europe and further afield. Nearer home, Edinburgh too was undergoing great changes, with the growth of the professions, particularly the legal one, leading to the creation of much wealth. The Old Town, or Auld Reekie as it was better known, was bursting at the seams and beginning to overflow.

All of these factors meant that people who hitherto had lived, or rather survived, in a largely self-sufficient rural economy were now flocking to towns to reap the benefits conferred by industrial and commercial growth, and somehow the food for them had to be found. The landowners soon realised the role which was expected of them: they had to improve their estates so that food production could keep pace with growth in demand from the cities and towns, in the process adding greatly to their income. But first they had to create the means of improving road communications so that vital commodities such as lime could be taken to their land, then to transport the produce to the markets where it would be needed. As packhorses were no longer appropriate to move large supplies, it would be necessary to create roads capable of taking cart-loads of material over long distances.

On the social side, the Scottish land-owning gentry were becoming aware of the lure of life now available to them in London and elsewhere, a magnet which was proving very strong. There were two impediments; the fact that their incomes generally from land were quite low compared with their more favoured counterparts in England and, on a very practical level, it was exceedingly difficult to travel to London (or anywhere else for that matter) with the appalling state of the roads.

Writing in his book *Life of Scotland in the Eighteenth Century*, H. G. Graham gives a graphic account of the problems encountered by Scottish gentry:

> *The nobleman driving in his lumbering coach brought over from Holland had two men to stand behind, armed with long poles for use when the vehicle capsized in some deep rut or over a large stone. The "running footman" with a staff, went on in front to see that the road was clear and as the coach with six horses slowly proceeded his difficulty was not to keep pace with it but to avoid far outstripping it so as to lose sight of it. In a more moderate style, the laird when he went a journey, he took with him one of his labouring men, who rode behind carrying the cloak bag; the ladies rode on pillions or on their own hags, a bag or little portmanteau easily containing their simple wardrobe for a visit.'*

What were the impediments to agricultural progress? Obviously the run-rig system and the primitive methods had to be done away with and a much better road network was vital. The initiative for these changes rested firmly with the landowners themselves, for any improvements could only enhance their own positions. Until now many of them were in the habit of staying at home due to the wretched condition of the roads. Graham again:

The highways were tracks of mire in wet weather and marshes in summer till the frosts made them sheets of ice, covered with drifting snow. When rain fell, the flat ground became lakes with islands of stone and the declavities became cataracts. Even towns were often connected by nothing more than pack-roads on which horses stumbled perilously along and carriages could not pass at all, over unenclosed land and moorland where, after rain, it was difficult to trace any beaten track.'

One of the first things which had to be done was to increase the fertility of the soil by adding lime, a mineral in very short supply in the Borders. The predominant acid soils of the area meant that crop roots did not grow satisfactorily and the introduction of lime neutralised the soil and supplied the major nutrient calcium. In the few favourable places locally with limestone outcrops, attempts had been made to extract it, but with very limited success. It was plentiful though further south in England and it was from there that small supplies had come by pack-horse; a laborious process which must have been of very limited success. So the need for wheeled vehicles was becoming paramount, especially as there was a growing demand for coal to replace the dwindling peat reserves as many of the moors and wastes were being brought into a productive state.

Delays in implementing enclosures were inevitable and even by the middle of the 18th century very few landowners in the Borders had begun the process, enclosure normally being restricted to the land immediately adjacent to their houses. But by 1760 changes were becoming more apparent and progress more rapid.

Later in the century and extending into the next, many of the properties changed hands, leading to the creation of smaller estates by successful merchants, colonial adventurers, lawyers and military men who were promoting themselves to landed status. In Roxburghshire between 1760 and 1815, two-thirds of the county changed hands in this fashion.

During this period, farms in today's familiar pattern were beginning to appear as were many of the villages which acted as focal points for the countryside. At the same time, many of the towns were being rebuilt as well. Decent accommodation for the farm workers took a while longer (although some lairds had made a start to provide housing for them), but for the greater part it would be well into the 19th century before the lure of town life and the resultant retreat from farm-working forced many landowners to build proper dwellings in an attempt to retain their workers.

Some of the local landowners adopted very positive attitudes towards land improvement and the people who worked on it. The Dukes of Buccleuch in particular had a sound altruistic approach to their tenants, in many instances dividing tracts of land into small areas to provide enough for a family. Later in the century, this went as far the provision of an entirely new town in Liddesdale, originally called Copshawholm and now known as Newcastleton. At Mellerstain in Berwickshire, the Earl of Haddington was one of the first to carry out improvements and he made a novel but successful experiment in bringing into his estate skilled farmers from already developed areas of England.

Tree planting started, one of the first to do so being the Duke of Roxburghe at his new home at Floors, Kelso in 1715. Lesser landlords too made their own contribution: Cockburn of Ormiston first introduced turnips to the Borders in 1725 and later in Melrose in 1747, Dr. John Rutherford, caused much excitement by growing them and having them fed to bullocks which became so fat compared with the normal stunted creatures that the people refused to eat the monsters. Potatoes were first grown in Chirnside as a field crop in 1740 but they had been introduced earlier by Lord Stair in 1724; by 1750 they were probably a universal crop grown in suitable soils throughout the area. James Dickson, one of the colonial adventurers, had returned to Kelso and about 1764 acquired the Ednam Estate, drained the lands there and rebuilt the village.

By the end of the century, most of the Merse of Berwickshire and the valleys of the Tweed and Teviot in Roxburghshire had been enclosed and made productive. This had been achieved by the landowners who were already getting together to take a close look at what must be done to improve the roads.

Chapter 5

Turnpike Roads

Various acts had been introduced by the Scottish Parliament in the 17th century in an attempt to improve roads, but none of them had much effect at that time. The Act of 1669 for Repairing Highways and Bridges introduced statute labour for the care of roads and bridges but was not brought into use until much later. It provided for twenty feet wide roads suitable for horses and carts and the intention was that the local heritors were empowered so that their tenants and servants could work on the roads, each for six days per year, compulsory and unpaid - the so called 'parish road days'.

It was not until the 1730s that the act came into play when the care of highways and bridges was placed in the hands of the sheriff of each county, with heritors being taxed for road works, this land tax or cess being fixed by locally-appointed commissioners of supply. These commissioners were usually all local landowners and as the statute labour was done parish by parish with little co-operation between neighbours, it was not surprising that the resultant piecemeal effect did very little for the roads or the travelling public using them.

About 1770 this labour was commuted into money which was used to employ proper workmen under competent supervision to make and repair roads in the summer months, the typical charge being 3d per day. To achieve this, separate acts were required county by county or even sometimes parish by parish and instead of commissioners of supply, the responsibility lay with trustees, often the same people - the local landowners.

Many of those who benefited from improved roads were outsiders and they paid nothing for helping to destroy the roads they used. The idea of charging tolls so that travellers helped to pay for road upkeep was not new; it was common in the continent and in England a toll had been exacted since 1663 on a heavily used part of the Great North Road, although it was only in 1696 when acts were being actively sought which led to a boom in the 1720s.

In Scotland, progress was much slower; the traffic to justify tolls simply did not exist until well into the mid-1700s, and it was only in 1751 that an act was passed by the Westminster Parliament which enabled turnpikes to be set up in Scotland.

The expression 'turnpike' derives from the use of a frame consisting of two cross-bars armed with pikes, which turned on a post and originally used by armies as a means of defence against attacking cavalry. This became considerably modified for civilian use and usually consisted of a timber arm which was free to swing through ninety degrees to bar a highway, or rested on a post on one side of the road and fitted with a counterbalanced weight on the other side, pivoted so that it could be raised or lowered at will under the control of the gatekeeper. In no time at all, highways so barred were referred to as 'turnpike' roads and often the road itself was referred to as 'the turnpike'. In turn the place where the barrier was installed became known as a toll or toll-house and the attendant the tollhouse-keeper or sometimes tacksman.

Another name for a toll was 'bar' but this was often reserved for those designed primarily for the passage of driven animals, often as 'side-bar', next to the toll for wheeled traffic. Tolls have long since gone from the Borders scene, but have been perpetuated in place-names such as Lamberton Toll just north of Berwick and Carter Bar on the road south of Jedburgh, both on the Northumberland border.

Tolls on bridges (known as 'pontage') were quite common before the coming of turnpike roads and was often used to repay the capital expenditure on construction, after which (in theory at any rate) they would be discontinued. Unlike ordinary tolls, they applied to pedestrians as well as animals and vehicles, so capturing everyone. Individual bridges were often later included with the relevant road in turnpike acts.

Heritors had to apply to parliament for a special act to enable them to go ahead with their own turnpike scheme. Permission was granted for a period of 21 years after which a further act would be needed. These turnpike acts established trusts and often at the same time allowed for the commutation of statute labour to deal with those roads in the area which were not being turnpiked. The right to manage turnpike trusts was, like statute labour, vested in heritors whose property valuation was high enough to allow them to assume this role but in general the trustees were those through whose estates the particular turnpike ran. Parliament stipulated that tolls could not be charged until the road had been sufficiently improved, but the standards varied enormously. The trusts met regularly, keeping minutes of all decisions, and ensuring that the rents from the tolls were accounted for and properly used for the provision of labour and materials on the roads as well for paying the surveyor and clerk/treasurer.

Many of the minutes from individual trusts have been preserved at the Selkirk Record Office and these, although tediously written by today's standards, they do give a flavour of the period. For example, at an 1808 meeting held in Kelso of the trust for the road from Lauder, the people attending were

Sir George Douglas, Bart. of Springwood Park (presiding)
Sir Henry Hay Makdougal, Bart. of Makerston
George Waldie of Hendersyde
Robert Walker of Wooden
Hugh Scott of Harden
James Potts, Writer in Kelso – Clerk and Treasurer
Robert Robertson of Sprouston – Surveyor.

The only major owner of land within miles of Kelso missing from the list was the Duke of Roxburghe, the reason being that at that time there had been a dispute concerning the succession to the title. A similar ring of landowners for each trust ensured, fairly or otherwise, that nothing was being done without their knowledge. They sometimes used their powerful positions to make things easier and more private for themselves by moving or deviating roads away from their own estates, an instance of this being at Manderston near Duns where the road to Chirnside takes a broad sweep to the south to avoid the grounds. Some owners had done this much earlier when estates were first being laid out in the early days of the 18th century; places like Castlecraig at Kirkurd near Blyth Bridge, Floors at Kelso and Mellerstain near Gordon.

At least at first, there would have been insufficient revenue from the tolls to meet incurred costs and usually money had to be borrowed against future income. Often trusts were burdened with debt and had great difficulty carrying out much work at all.

The right to collect tolls was let annually and the business of collection and profit was left to the tacksman at each toll. Occasionally one person was successful in making bids for a number of lettings and these were then sub-let, an example of this being at Selkirkshire where one tenant held Sunderland, Shawburn and Selkirk itself. Lettings were from May to May and advertisements appeared in local newspapers in the spring.

For some of the better-used tolls, competition for these lettings became brisk at the roups which were held at appropriate towns and often this meant that potential toll tenants stretched themselves by overbidding, almost inevitably leading to default and bankruptcy.

In many other cases, the tollkeepers resorted to other means of income as well, the commonest being the sale of liquor, which although illegal without a licence, was commonly done under the eye of the authorities, despite complaints by innkeepers and the clergy. Some tollkeepers did manage to get a liquor licence and in such cases it was customary to increase the rent by about 10%. Places on the border with England found another way of generating income by marrying runaway couples, a function commonly associated with Gretna Green in neighbouring Dumfriesshire, but carried out with vigour at Lamberton Toll near Berwick and at Coldstream Bridge. Most of the trustees seemed to turn a blind eye to these extra-mural activities provided they received enhanced rents.

To start with, not many new roads were created in the Borders; in most cases improvements were made to the old ones by adding stones (often from river beds) to create a ridge supported by larger stones to prevent scattering. In practice these roads were often unsatisfactory, for heavy wheeled vehicles such as carriages and carts tended to push the small stones to one side despite the heavier ones, so creating ruts which could be very difficult to negotiate, especially if no drainage arrangements had been made. Despite these difficulties, few people thought that a turnpike was any worse than what it had replaced. As will be seen in chapter 17, it was only much later with Telford and McAdam and their radical ideas that road building had its real boost.

Some of the earliest acts to improve the roads were those of 1753 for the stretch from the head of the Tweed to Edinburgh via Blyth Bridge, 1762 for Coldstream Bridge and attendant roads, 1768 for Lauder to Carter Bar and from Crosslee to Haremoss south of Selkirk on the Edinburgh to Carlisle road.

It was soon apparent that it was uneconomic to run all the separate turnpike trusts individually and it was not long before they were being amalgamated, so sharing experience as well as office-bearers and surveyors. By the 1850s, this resulted in their number being reduced to six:

Berwickshire Roads Trust – divided into three divisions: Lauder, Middle based on Duns and Eastern based at Ayton. Coldstream Bridge Toll was always dealt with separately.

Kelso Union Turnpike Trust – divided into three districts, west, north and south, covering most of the northern part of Roxburghshire.

Selkirk and St.Boswells Turnpike Trust – despite the title, most of the roads were actually in southern Roxburghshire, and it was based on Hawick.

Roxburgh Turnpike Trust – based at Jedburgh and covering the balance of the county.

Selkirkshire and Ettrick Turnpike Roads Trust.

Peeblesshire Turnpike Trust.

When tolls were first introduced, some towns had them built to cover almost every entrance, despite the fact that the roads had not yet been improved. In Jedburgh for example, there were at least six toll-gates in 1775 but it was not long before this was reduced to two. This happened in other places too, but records are often very scanty. In all there were about 200 tolls throughout the Borders, but many of these had replaced other earlier ones and some had been closed when roads were moved. By 1840 there were only about 95 in operation and after that the number dropped considerably as efforts were made to find other systems of collecting money for road maintenance.

The Scottish Turnpike Act of 1831 tidied up some of the fragmented laws which previously applied. For instance, funerals were now exempted from tolls in the parish of the deceased. Later, in 1850, tolls and pontages were abolished for all funerals and their attendants. This gave rise to a sudden but perhaps unsurprising increase in the number of persons claiming exemption from tolls because they said they were on their way to and from such sombre events.

Generally, driven beasts were on hill tracks (the drove roads) and it was only at unavoidable river crossings such as Romanno Bridge that the drovers were obliged to pay. Even then some successfully detoured round the tolls, often with the connivance of local small farmers who, like many others, had little love for the turnpike system. At Clackmae Toll on the old Jedburgh Road west of Earlston, the farmer there was accused of permitting led animals to bypass the toll by allowing the drovers to use the fields on either side.

In Berwickshire there were a number of trouble-spots - the Duns area was turnpiked in 1791-2 and there was great opposition to the seven toll-bars, two of which were in the town itself. Almost as soon as the tolls had been erected, the town ones were destroyed by fire and soon afterwards two in the countryside were also wrecked. This could not have done much for the confidence of the tollhouse-keepers who saw their anticipated incomes disappearing, especially the woman who was in sole charge of the Paxton toll on the English border. It appears that the tolls in Duns were never replaced.

These ill-feelings were often widespread and sometimes a plan to build a new toll had to be abandoned for fear of unrest from the local population - this happened in 1811 at an unknown site on the Lauder to Kelso road.

As late as 1854, Kelso bridge saw serious rioting because of an allegation by townsfolk that they were being forced to pay pontage after the bridge costs had been met from the tolls; the resultant pitched battle almost led to the destruction of the toll-house. Later a successful prosecution was taken against the bridge trustees for what was seen as exploitation. In chapter 8 it will be shown how a similar practice was exposed at Coldstream by no less a figure than Thomas Telford when he prepared his report on the proposed new mailcoach road through the town. In that case the townspeople seemed unaware that there was no obligation for them to continue to pay tolls on the bridge as the capital costs had already been repaid.

Tollhouses were built in all shapes and sizes and a diminishing number survive today, although most of them have now been modified or extended. Often they were based on a normal dwelling house, either with windows at each side or a projecting porch in front with side windows; all so that there was a clear view of the road in either direction. Often too they were designed specifically to meet a local need such as being at a junction, an instance of this type may still be seen at West Linton. A most unusual polygonal one is at Greenbank near Roberton. Here two corners of the building on the road give the appearance of having been lopped off and on the faces thus exposed, windows have been inserted to allow for good views up and down the road.

As they had to be at the side of the highway, many of the tolls were casualties of road-widening schemes in this century. One of the last to be affected was that between St. Boswells and Newtown St. Boswells on the A68 which had to be demolished some years ago to make way for the new bypass.

When new roads were built then the tolls on the old roads were closed and sometimes compensation had to be paid if this occurred in the middle of a rental period. When the Mertoun bridge was completed on the new road between St. Boswells and Kelso in 1841, this had a serious effect on the income of the tollkeeper on the Teviot Bridge at Kelso and he had to be compensated. Similarly the toll-keeper at Sunderland and Selkirk on the old road northwards from that town was given relief for loss when the new road from Galashiels was completed in 1833.

There were no hard rules about where toll-houses should be set up, but county boundaries were nearly always chosen and sometimes there was one on either side. Where a trust had originally been created for one road, then usually there would have been tolls at either end and probably several in between – all waiting to relieve the traveller of his money. If there had been pontage on a bridge prior to the road being turnpiked, then this usually continued. Many of the new bridges created by turnpike trusts were also made subject to tolls and these were invariably unpopular as they applied to pedestrians as well as riders and horse-drawn vehicles. Almost everywhere, the pontage charge for pedestrians was one penny.

A typical turnpike act stated the approximate route of the proposed highway and the reason for it - often words to the effect that '*it is always impassable for coaches, wagons and other carriages and dangerous for persons travelling on horseback*'. Then it went on in great detail to describe the legal niceties involved and the means of raising the proposed tolls. Usually frustratingly missing was an accurate route description and the whereabouts of the proposed toll-gates.

In 1765 when the early turnpike acts were being put through parliament, a typical set of charges read as follows:-

For each coach, landau, chariot, Berlin, chaise, hearse, wagon, wain, cart, sledge and other carriage:-	
drawn by 6 or more horses, mules or other beasts of draught	1s6d
drawn by 4 horses, etc.	1s
drawn by 2 horses, etc.	6d
Mounted horses	1^1/$_2$d
Horses, led	1d
Cattle	10d per score
Calves, sheep, lambs and hogs	2^1/$_2$d per score

Although inflation was not usually an important factor in those days, the Napoleonic Wars appear to have had a dramatic effect on these costs. When one act was renewed in 1808, all the above prices were doubled and this probably applied to most of the others as well.

Tickets were usually available for return journeys and sometimes there were reduced rates for the vital commodities of lime and coal. Occasionally it was possible to arrange with the trustees for a special pass, something which would be called a season ticket today. Before Selkirk had its own railway service, George Dryden operated an omnibus coach from there to Galashiels station and he negotiated with the Selkirkshire Trustees for an annual amount of £120 to obtain freedom from toll duties between the towns.

There were several important exceptions to the payment of tolls; generally the following categories did not have to pay:-

Animals or carts carrying road-making materials
Ministers of religion in their own parishes
Military traffic
Vagrants.

Mailcoaches were treated differently, for by an act of parliament they were exempt from paying tolls from 1785, one year before the first mailcoach actually appeared in Scotland. Turnpike trustees saw a valuable source of income being denied them and there were many campaigns to have the act repealed. This met with no success in England, but the Scottish trustees were much more fortunate, for north of the border that act was repealed in 1813, so that mail carriages with more than two wheels had to pay the required toll charge. To compensate the Post Office for this drain on their income, each letter in Scotland carried on such coaches was surcharged with an additional half-penny – naturally causing uproar amongst those engaged in correspondence.

Although tolls were normally to be found along turnpike roads, there were a few exceptions to this rule in the Borders. In Peeblesshire there were two on the boundary with Midlothian, the first at Tweeddaleburn on a minor road between Eddleston and Temple, marked in the 1775 map as the way to Dalkeith. The second was at Scarcerig near Cockmuir Farm east of Leadburn on another road to Dalkeith which now exists only as a footpath.

In Berwickshire, two roads which crossed the Tweed into England had pontage tolls on them despite the fact that neither road appeared to have been turnpiked. The tolls were at Ladykirk near the Norham Bridge and at the Union Bridge near Horncliffe.

Sometimes neighbouring trusts resorted to squabbling with one another over toll income. Galashiels Damhead Bar, erected in 1849 on the road to Peebles, was one of the last tolls to be built in the Borders and although most of Galashiels was in Selkirkshire, an odd quirk meant that at that time the toll itself was actually in Roxburghshire. The Selkirkshire turnpike trustees tried very hard to secure a substantial part of the tolls for themselves; their counterparts in Roxburghshire were reminded of this at least once a year but there is no record that anything ever came of it

With the arrival of the railways, the income from many of the tolls suffered badly. In Selkirkshire for example, the annual letting fees dropped dramatically between 1836 (prior to the railways) and 1858, nine years after the opening of the main line from Edinburgh through Galashiels but only two years from the start of the branch service to Selkirk. The following shows this clearly:-

Toll	1836 Fees	1858 Fees
Sunderland, Shawburn and Selkirk (one tenant)	£374	£135
Crosslie	307	18
Ladyland	241	Not let
Thornilee	58	45

Thornilee on the Peebles road was the only toll where the drop was not catastrophic, but this was because the railway line from Peebles to Galashiels was not completed until 1866.

Because of the effect of the railways, from 1864 there started to be a move away from tolls, the money to maintain roads being raised from a uniform assessment on land and heritages. This was the precursor to what generally became known as the rating system, later expanded to include other local services such as housing, education and the police when these responsibilities were transferred to the new County Councils in 1895.

In Selkirkshire, their turnpike act expired in 1865 and they were the first in the Borders to use the new method. The trustees had calculated a rate of 5d. in the pound levied on a valuation roll of all property in the county (including that of the railways) to enable them to meet the estimated expenditure of £1522 on their roads, including those previously dealt with by statute labour. At the same time, all the toll-houses in the county were closed. Other trusts seemed to carry on as before for some time and in Kelso for example the minutes recorded that as late as 1872 tolls were still being gathered.

The official end of the turnpike system came with the passing of the Roads and Bridges Act of 1883.

Chapter 6

The Great North Road (A1)

Map 5

This was one of the better known roads in Britain, although in its early life it must have been quite difficult to see where the 'great' part had come from. But it was the road from London to Edinburgh through Berwick and for years it conjured up all sorts of romantic ideas in the minds of travellers, both the real and armchair variety. The reality was very different though, for at least in Berwickshire it ran through some bleak moorland, with precipitous ravines to negotiate before reaching the comparative safety of the Lothians.

It was probably the route of the first coach into Scotland, that of a somewhat courageous English Ambassador to the Scottish Court who in 1596 travelled in this way to Edinburgh from London to take up his appointment. It would be many years before another attempt was made to take a coach over the border.

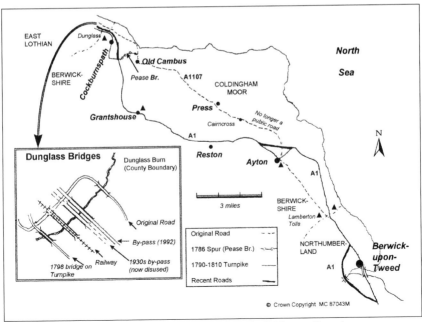

Map 5 – The Great North Road, with inset showing the bridges at Dunglass.

The road ran north-west from Berwick, entered Scotland just south of Lamberton and crossed lonely Lamberton Moor to Ayton. It continued on what are now farm-tracks until Cairncross and along a road (which still exists) to cross the feared Coldingham Moor. On the moor it passed Press, later to become the site of a well-known inn and posting-house in the early days of coaches.

Shortly afterwards, still continuing in the same direction, the way followed part of today's Coldingham to Cockburnspath road (A1107) until the hamlet of Old (or Auld) Cambus was reached. From here much of the old road has been destroyed, but traces of it reappear just before the steep decline into the Pease Burn which is crossed by a ford close to the seashore. The ford still remains, one of the few left on public roads in the Borders, although the road on it is not a busy one except in the holiday season. The incline afterwards is almost as bad as the way down and although modern vehicles have no difficulty in using these narrow roads, motorists may find it hard to imagine how the first coaches, on poor unsurfaced tracks, ever made it past this natural barrier.

From here things improved, the road still maintaining the same general north-westerly direction, passing close by Cove on the coast and Cockburnspath inland. The latter village became an important stopping place and staging post for travellers and a very early inn was established there, thought to have been on the same site as today's hotel. Within a mile to the north of the village, the Dunglass Burn runs to the sea in a deep ravine to form the boundary between East Lothian and Berwickshire. The difficulty of traversing this ravine was resolved very early by the construction of a narrow ancient bridge which still exists and may be walked over. People today do so, perhaps without realising it, for the trees in the ravine have grown so high on either side that it is by no means obvious that one is on a bridge at all.

From here the road carried on through Dunbar and Haddington then Tranent and Musselburgh on its way to Edinburgh. The entire length within Berwickshire is just short of twenty miles.

Prior to 1603, a track of a kind had existed but certainly it would never have been intended for wheeled vehicles. Apart from the occasional traveller, its obvious use might have been to assist armies on their marauding ways north and south but (as mentioned in Chapter 3) this did not happen very often, the Soutra way being the preferred one. It should have been the obvious way for Edward II on his return to England after his defeat at Bannockburn in 1314, but instead he went by boat from Dunbar – perhaps considered less risky that tackling the ravines of Berwickshire.

When the Earl of Hertford came this way after sacking and burning Edinburgh in 1544, he reported on the defile at the Pease Burn with the comment '*The passage was such that having no let* (hindrance) *it was three hours before all the army could pass it*'. This may give some indication of what a lengthy process it was to traverse the ravine. It would have taken longer if the opposition he expected at the neighbouring strongholds at Cockburnspath Tower and Dunglass Castle had materialised.

In 1603 the road saw an historic ride from London to Edinburgh, one made by Robert Carey who carried the news of the death of Queen Elizabeth of England to James VI of Scotland in his palace at Holyrood. The journey of almost 400 miles took him sixty hours, a very impressive time considering the state of the road and a serious fall which caused a badly injured arm. The news had not been unexpected, nor was the message that James had been proclaimed king of two realms, additionally becoming James I south of the border. Carey (later to become Earl of Monmouth) was no stranger to the Borders through which his ride took him, for he had at one time or another been the Warden of all three English Marches during the worst days of reiving.

After a week of urgent preparations James departed for his new kingdom and capital, accompanied by a large retinue of family, courtiers and hangers-on. At Berwick he was very concerned with the poor condition of the ramshackle wooden bridge over the Tweed and it was perhaps because of this that work started on a solid stone bridge which still stands today. Soon the road was becoming quite busy with the traffic of regal letters and documents and this inevitably led to a demand for a courier service for civilian letters, so creating the germ of the first postal communication north of the border.

When James left Edinburgh, he promised to return frequently, but in fact he only came back once in 1617 and everyone involved in his visit would probably have agreed that this had been enough. In preparation for the journey, considerable improvements were carried out on the Ayton to Cockburnspath stretch of the Great North Road (which certainly was a benefit for the local population) but on the debit side, Berwickshire was almost bankrupted by the royal demands for assistance to see his entourage safely through the county.

First of all he requisitioned for stages to be set up on the Great North Road so that horses could be changed. This meant a large army of men had to be found from somewhere merely to help with the horses en route and see to fodder. But much worse was to come, for next he demanded the following number of horses to be supplied from these places:

Greenlaw	37	Polworth	13
Gordon	24	Hume	12
Bassingdane *(Bassendean)*	9	Earlston	25
Longformacus	4	Langton	24
Dunse *(Duns)*	20	Lauder	36
Chingilkirk *(Channelkirk)*	13	Fogo	24
Mairton *(Merton)*	20	Stitchil *(Stichill)*	25
Kelso	50		

This total of 336 horses would have been a trying demand for such a small county and perhaps was the reason why they had to go further afield to places like Kelso and Stichill in neighbouring Roxburghshire. It is believed that there may have been over five thousand in the king's train by the time it arrived at Berwick from the south, so the need for all these horses becomes apparent. To the relief of folk in Berwickshire, the King returned to England by way of Carlisle.

People started to travel between the capitals in ever-increasing numbers after the Union in 1707; Scottish members of parliament attending Westminster for the first time, a host of civil servants, businessmen from both countries looking for opportunities in the new climate now pervading, members of the newly-emerging middle-classes who had heard so much about the delights of London and travellers from the south driven north by curiosity to see what this strange wild country north of the border looked like.

Most of this travelling had either to be done on horseback or by sea (there was a steady flow of shipping between places like Leith and the south) and this led to a mounting pressure for improvements to the road. Stagecoaches had been used, but only in the summer months and failures were more common than successes. What was wanted was a way of overcoming the dangerous Pease Burn and, until this was done, it was unlikely that proper coach services would be available.

High-level viaducts had just become fashionable when David Henderson of Edinburgh was asked to produce plans for a bridge to cross the Pease ravine at a point just half a mile upstream from the ford. When it was completed in 1786 it consisted of four brick arches and stood about 130 feet above the water, making it for a while the highest bridge in the world. Its elegance was enhanced by cylindrical voids of nine feet in diameter which pierced the structure between the curves of the arches, the intention being to lighten the weight. The bridge was connected to the former road which now ran westwards from a point close to Old Cambus, over the new bridge and on by a new route to nearby Cockburnspath.

Just as at Dunglass further up the road, the ravine at Pease has become filled with tall trees, making it difficult to get a good sight of this impressive bridge.

Pease Bridge, Berwickshire, built in 1786. (from an engraving)

The same year as the bridge was finished, the first daily stagecoaches ran between Edinburgh and London with a journey time of sixty hours; something unheard of before. Horses were changed only once in Berwickshire, at the Press Inn, which lay 14 miles south of Dunbar and 12 miles from the next stage at Berwick. There was also a post office there for most of the early coach period, this having replaced the original one at Cockburnspath.

Road users were still not satisfied with the road, for the narrow Dunglass Bridge posed great problems for the coaches and the notorious Coldingham Moor was feared by all, being described in 1793 as the most dangerous part of the road between Edinburgh and London. A turnpike trust for the moor stretch of the road had been authorised as far back as 1772 but the money derived from the commutation of statute labour was insufficient to create a new road; it being only enough to try to contain the worst aspects of the existing one which in a period of twenty years had used up the then enormous amount of £3,000. Clearly something else was needed and pressure was exerted from all sides, not least the General Post Office which had a vested interest in speeding up the mails.

The outcome was a survey of the entire road between Edinburgh and Newcastle via Berwick, carried out in the 1790s. The first action was taken with a new bridge to cross the Dunglass Burn to replace the old narrow one. Completed in 1798, this is a further example of fine bridge-building which appears to have been a characteristic of the period.

But this was only a start – a mere hors d'œuvre for the main work, an entirely new road from south of Cockburnspath to follow the valley of the Eye Water to Ayton. It passed close to Reston and further up the valley a new hamlet grew up around an inn thought to have been started by Thomas Grant, a Highlander who worked on the road and opened an ale-house to serve his fellow workers. At first this was called Tommy Grant's, but soon the inn and the hamlet became known as Grantshouse, and so called today although the road no longer passes by the front door of the hotel.

The new road met the old one again at Ayton and much road realignment had to take place there, requiring almost a remodelling of the layout of the village. From there it went towards the sea to avoid Lamberton Moor and joined the old road once more close to the border with Northumberland, then into Berwick and over the 17th century bridge there. Much of the work was done in short stretches and it took several years before final completion about 1810.

The road was never far from the Eye Water (nor indeed was the later railway which followed roughly the same course on its way southwards to Berwick in 1845/6) and shows clearly how ground drainage control of the waterways had at last enabled road-builders to use these easier river valleys, whereas before they were debarred because of the marshy ground and the constant threat of flooding. The latest methods of road-building had been used, including those advocated by John McAdam, to produce the first real attempt at a modern highway in the Borders.

Shortly after the new road was finally completed, the inn and post-office at Press were closed. The latter was transferred back to Cockburnspath which saw a comparative rise in prosperity now that it had been selected for staging both mail and passenger coaches. The Pease Bridge had a short life serving the Great North Road – after only 24 years the road on it was relegated to serve only local traffic.

In the 1820s the entire stretch of the Great North Road northwards from Newcastle was surveyed by Thomas Telford, contracted by the Government on behalf of the Postmaster General to assess whether this was the best route for mails to and from Edinburgh. Although his report (see chapter 17) came out in favour of the way by Coldstream, a compromise was reached so that the day mail continued to use the Great North Road, but Coldstream would gain the night one.

As with other roads throughout the country, much of the importance of the Great North Road diminished severely with the arrival of the railways. What had been the pinnacle of success for roads in the 1830s became a plateau in the next two decades and a long decline for the remainder of the century. It was in the 20th century with motorised transport that the road once again came into prominence.

Just as with other major routes, it was taken over in the 1930s by the Ministry of Transport under new Trunk Road provisions and the responsibility for its maintenance and repair passed from Berwick County Council to the Scottish Office. Slightly earlier, road classification and numbering came into use when the Great North Road became the A1, reflecting the importance of the route linking the two capitals.

Inevitably parts of the new road have had to be altered to meet the demands of the sheer volume of modern traffic on this major trunk-route. In the 1930s, a new bridge was built at Dunglass near the 1798 one and this in turn was closed in 1992 when yet a further one was constructed to accommodate the Cockburnspath by-pass. This has produced the unusual sight of five bridges crossing the burn, all within a quarter-mile of one another, four for roads (of which two still carry traffic) and the other carrying the main railway line. About twenty years ago, Ayton village was bypassed.

Across the border in Berwick a massive concrete structure known as The Royal Tweed Bridge was built in 1928 to take the traffic away from the old one. A much-needed bypass for Berwick was completed in 1984 necessitating a further bridge, so bringing into being the A1 trunk road as we know it today. For most of its way in England, the A1 is dual-carriageway (some of it to motorway standards) but in Berwickshire, so far only a short stretch has been completed. Nearer Edinburgh, further improvements are continuing.

Coaching Inns

When the first coaches were struggling along the Great North Road, the only post-house on the way was at Cockburnspath. This was where the earliest messengers had changed horses and it became the first post office in the Borders in 1693. It went out of favour when the Press Inn was opened but re-emerged in 1813 shortly after the new road was completed. From then it went from strength to strength, handling all coach traffic (including the mails) from Edinburgh to Berwick and on to London. From these humble beginnings it developed into today's Cockburnspath Hotel, lying at the edge of the village and on the main road until the bypass was built in 1992.

The Press Inn was also well known, for it must have been a haven in the midst of the wastes of Coldingham Moor. The post office there opened in 1768 and when the mailcoaches started in 1786, it was at the Press Inn that horses were changed and the mailbag for Duns taken off. It was closed in 1813 shortly after the opening of the new road was completed. Now all traces of this old inn have disappeared, but until a few years ago there was a small building standing next to the road, known locally as the old Parcel Office.

Hostelries sprang up along the road at Grantshouse and nearby Renton, Houndwood and Reston as well as at Ayton (Red Lion), but none managed to capture the lucrative stagecoach and mailcoach trade as coaching inns.

Across the border, Berwick had at least three important coaching-inns, two of them still there. The largest and most important was the King's Arms in Hide Hill, one of the most imposing inns on the Great North Road and still operating as a hotel today. The second, also still there, was the Hen and Chickens, in a building converted into an inn about 1790 in Sandgate at the foot of Hide Hill. The third inn has now gone; it was the Red Lion in Marygate, on the site of the present Woolworth's store. All three inns served most of the traffic on the Great North Road in addition to the coaches for such inland places as Wooler and Kelso.

Tolls

There were four tolls on the road, two of them being at the extremities of the Borders. At the northern end to serve the boundary with East Lothian there was Dunglass, not near the bridge of the same name, but half-way to Cockburnspath. The second was at Grantshouse (close to the inn there) and the third at the southern end of the village of Ayton. In the south the final one was on the national boundary with England at Lamberton. When the route was changed to the present one early in the 19th century, Old Lamberton toll was closed and a new one erected. Lamberton toll, like the one at Coldstream, was used for the marriage of runaway couples and this lucrative activity for the toll-keepers was transferred over as well when the traffic moved to the new road.

Chapter 7

The Way over Soutra (A68)

Map 6

The Lammermuir road by Soutra into the Borders from the north was and is used by so many routes that this chapter has been devoted to it. From Edinburgh, the way has always been by Dalkeith, Pathhead and Fala.

The name Soutra often means something special to Borderers, for it marks their northern boundary: going in that direction, it is the first opportunity to see the broad sweep of the Lothians from west to east, the Firth of Forth, beyond it the hills of Fife and on a clear day the outline of far-away mountains behind Stirling. At that distance the city of Edinburgh appears merely as a large dark patch under the brooding Arthur's Seat. But often of much more importance to many Borderers is on their return journey homewards, when from Soutra they have the first endearing sight of the Borders - the broad stretch of Lauderdale leading to a glimpse of the Eildon Hills and beyond them the long ridge of the Cheviot Hills.

In poor weather the Soutra road can be very dangerous and it therefore receives much publicity from weather forecasters and traffic reporters. The actual length of the road over the Lammermuir Hills is only about five miles but as it rises to just over one thousand feet, drivers have to contend with some horrific weather conditions - and not always in the heart of winter either. Gates have been erected at either end of the pass and these are closed when the weather deteriorates to the extent that it would become dangerous to proceed. Illuminated signs on the roads warn drivers of this and when it occurs, Borderers are effectively cut off from the north, unless they are prepared to make a considerable detour to the A7 through the Gala valley or the A1 coastal route.

Soutra takes its name from a modest hill of 1209 feet forming part of the Lammermuir range that creates a natural and geographical boundary between the Lothians and the Scottish Borders. The Romans made their road to the Forth past Soutra Hill and since that time until the eighteenth century the route created by Britannia's invaders has been the highway serving most of the central parts of Selkirkshire, Roxburghshire and Berwickshire.

In Anglo-Saxon times the road became known as Dere Street, reputedly *the way to the wild animals* and this name is still used to this day. That was not its only name

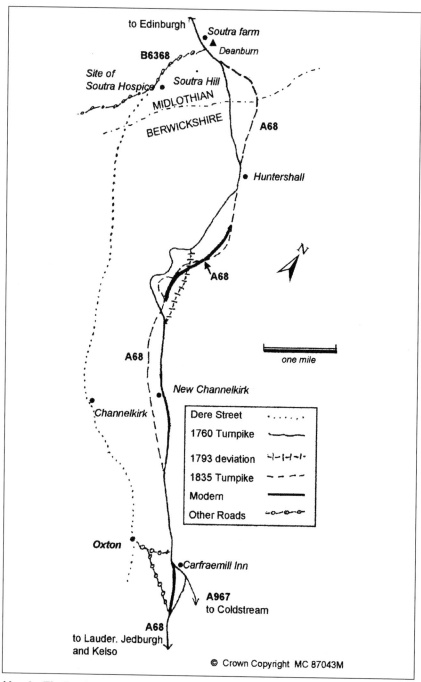

to Edinburgh

Soutra farm

Deanburn

B6368

Site of
Soutra Hospice

Soutra Hill

MIDLOTHIAN

BERWICKSHIRE

A68

Huntershall

A68

N

A68

one mile

New Channelkirk

Channelkirk

Dere Street	· · · · · · ·
1760 Turnpike	—
1793 deviation	-ı-ı-ı-ı-
1835 Turnpike	– – –
Modern	▬
Other Roads	-o-o-o-

Oxton

Carfraemill Inn

A967
to Coldstream

A68
to Lauder. Jedburgh
and Kelso

© Crown Copyright MC 87043M

Map 6 – The Roads over Soutra.

though, for it was also known as Gamiel's Path (at least in Northumberland but perhaps also in Scotland) and later as Malcolm's Road or the King's Road. Malcolm was only one of many kings who used this way to and from the hunting grounds of Ettrick Forest which covered most of Selkirkshire.

Armies made frequent use of Soutra: Edward I on his campaigns, Edward II on his way to defeat at Bannockburn, James II passed along it to his death by bursting cannon at Roxburgh, James III to his showdown with his barons at Lauder, James IV on his last journey to Flodden, James V to defeat on Solway Moss and finally Prince Charles Edward Stuart (Bonny Prince Charlie) on his way south to Derby in 1745. It has been estimated that in the course of its history, no fewer than eighty armies have trudged along this road on their way to and from hostilities.

In medieval times the main use of the road, as well as carrying armies and hunting monarchs, was for the passage of monks and other persons concerned with the activities of the Border abbeys. Just over the boundary into Midlothian a refuge had been created on a high point of the road as a stopping place for these monks, known as Soltra or Soutra Hospice. As its fame as a centre of healing spread, the buildings grew to cope with the increasing demand and in its heyday it became the principal hospital for the people of Edinburgh, despite being eighteen miles from the capital. The Reformation saw the end of the monks and Soutra Hospice and before long the buildings lay in ruins. Today all traces above ground level have gone and the only structure there now is Soutra Aisle, a 17th century burial vault.

Dere Street continued to be used as the principal road over the Lammermuir Hills, with little or no sophisticated repairs or maintenance being done to the Roman work. It lasted so long because the amount of wheeled traffic on it was very small; most of the users were on foot or on horseback. But it would have been quite unsuitable for the coaches and heavy carts being introduced in the 18th century, some of the gradients being too much for draught horses. Dere Street was essentially a ridgeway road when it crossed the hills, so avoiding the worst of the boggy areas lower down, but with a better knowledge of land drainage and river control, road designers began to see the merits of highways nearer the river basins to avoid steep gradients.

When the first turnpike roads were being planned from 1750 onwards, it was decided that Dere Street would have to be replaced by an easier route. This was achieved in the Turnpike Act of 1760, when the way agreed by the Trustees on both sides of the boundary was to go round the north side of Soutra Hill from the farm of the same name, on to moorland at Huntershall then to wend its way south into the steep valley of the Headshaw Burn, one of the feeder streams for the Leader Water. It went by the east bank of this burn until the Leader Water was joined then followed that until Carfraemill.

Carfraemill was to become an important junction, for it was from this point that the road divided; the eastward leg going to such places as Greenlaw, Duns and Coldstream and the westward to Lauder, Jedburgh and Kelso. These onward roads are dealt with in their respective chapters.

Halfway down the Headshaw valley, an inn called The New Channelkirk had been built to accommodate travellers. It replaced a similar establishment which had been on Dere Street.

The former New Channelkirk Inn built to serve traffic on the first turnpike road over Soutra constructed in 1760 to replace Dere Street. This old road is shown on the bottom left of the picture and is still in use as a farmtrack. Its replacement in 1835 (and now the A68) can be positioned by the line of traffic halfway up the distant slope.

There must have been difficulties in dealing with some of the gradients on the new road, for in 1793 a short alternative route was built where the land starts to fall sharply on the southern side. Presumably this helped to ease the passage of coaches and this route became a very popular one, in time taking much of the traffic originally destined to go by the Great North Road. The upsurge of traffic in the 1800s gave rise to demands for a better road and, as was so often the case, it was the General Post Office which put pressure on the trustees. Arising from this, Thomas Telford was appointed to survey the route and make recommendations. This he did in 1832, producing the first really accurate map of the road and its gradients. At the northern (Midlothian) end, he planned an entirely new route up to Soutra, skirting the hill in a much wider arc to ease the climb. The centre section at Huntershall was left in place, but as the road descended southwards, he avoided the steep upper Headshaw valley by proceeding higher up on the west bank to rejoin the original turnpike road about a mile north of Carfraemill. In his report, Telford emphasised that his plan would mean that the existing gradients of 1 in 9, 10 and 11 from the summit to the Channelkirk Inn would be replaced by more manageable ones of 1 in 22 and 24. These recommendations were accepted and work was started in 1835 to produce the road which for the most part is still with us today.

The new road meant the end of the New Channelkirk Inn, it being replaced by the one at the Carfraemill junction, now known as The Lodge. The buildings at New Channelkirk can still be seen lying in the Headshaw valley below the present road and now a private house. The first turnpike road has become a farm track and it shows all too clearly just how narrow it was. The Ordnance Survey *Pathfinder* 1:25000 map marks this track as the 'King's Road' but I doubt if this expression was ever used for a road built as late as 1760. That name probably died with the end of Dere Street as a public highway.

The one toll on this road was unusual in that although it was built and run to provide income for a Border Trust, it was actually situated at Deanburn in Midlothian, at least a mile north of the border-line. The obvious place for such a toll would have been at Huntershall, but perhaps great difficulty was found in finding a tollkeeper prepared to work at that isolated spot.

Apart from the inevitable widening of the road to cater for today's traffic demands, the most significant recent change is at the top of the Headshaw valley where modern engineering methods have permitted embankments and cuttings to provide greater relief from the gradients there. The way taken by Telford's road can still be seen, for these are now used as vehicle lay-bys on either side of the road. In recent times, to assist with road management and the improvement of safety, the junction at Carfraemill was first of all moved lightly westwards, then later was converted to a roundabout.

Chapter 8

The Edinburgh Road to Coldstream (A68 and A697)

Map 7

This road has been used by people and armies alike from medieval times. Armies found the ford at Coldstream a convenient crossing point over the Tweed and when the bridge was finally built there in 1766, part of the money came from government sources in an attempt to improve strategic crossing places in the event of a further Jacobite uprising.

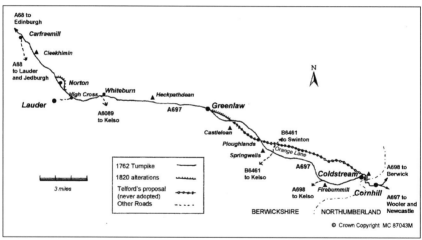

Map 7 – The Edinburgh Road to Coldstream.

As far as Carfraemill, the road from Edinburgh is the same as that used for traffic to Jedburgh (today's A68) and is dealt with in the previous chapter. From there it followed the way similar to today's main road except that then it passed by Norton Inn and nearby Drummonds Hall, both of which lie across the Leader from Lauder. At High Cross (where it met the ancient road to Kelso) it turned eastward past the settlement of Thirlstane near the site of the ruined castle which pre-dated the existing one at Lauder. It continued through Greenlaw and on to Coldstream. With only minor changes, the route taken by this road is the same as today's A697, a major highway between Edinburgh and Newcastle. At Coldstream, the ford was not at today's bridge but a little upstream near the confluence of the Tweed with the Leet. Halfway across the ford, they were in England and the village of Cornhill was only a short distance away.

The Turnpike Act of 1762 was intended to improve the roads around Coldstream to prepare for the bridge to be completed four years later and few alterations were made to the line of the road on its journey south of Carfraemill. But it was improved and bridges were built in place of the few fords along the way.

Coldstream bridge is one of the finest on the Tweed and the first 'modern' one, only the much-altered bridge at Peebles being older. Designed by James Smeaton for the Tweed Bridges Trust, it stands today virtually as it was built, the only change being the outward movement of the parapets to cater for the widening of the road surface in 1961. At the town end of the bridge the toll-house soon became famous for the Gretna-type weddings held here for runaway couples from England.

When the work was finally completed, the new route offered possibilities for an alternative way from Edinburgh to Newcastle via Wooler and Morpeth, avoiding the hazards of the Great North Road. Another important factor was that it was the shorter of the two: from London to Edinburgh via Berwick at that time was 386 miles, whereas by Wooler and Coldstream it was 372, a difference of fourteen miles.

In 1820 the General Post Office was keen to make use of this alternative route and a Parliamentary Select Committee had been set up to investigate. Thomas Telford was appointed to carry out a survey of the entire length and to make recommendations for improvement. Some of his suggestions were quite radical but few of them were actually accepted, due possibly to the costs involved - he estimated that these would total £9170 for work between Pathhead in Midlothian and Coldstream, a considerable sum in those days. Over Soutra, his recommendations were carried out (see Chapter 7), as was a most sensible deviation eastwards to avoid Norton Inn and Drummonds Hall and so overcome a dangerous hill near the latter.

Far more contentious but forward-looking was his plan to by-pass Coldstream altogether. In his report he referred to the road between Greenlaw and Coldstream Bridge being 'very crooked, passing over sundry hills to the westward of the town, whereas the bridge is considerably eastward'. What he proposed was an entirely new line of road starting at Greenlaw and proceeding more or less in a straight line towards the Coldstream direction, crossing the existing road at Ploughlands and passing close to Stainrigg and Hirsel Law at the top of the Hirsel estate. From there it turned towards the bridge, passing the farm at Coldstream Mains. Only a tiny part of this was ever carried out (a short section east of Greenlaw) and today many Coldstream people must wonder what the town would be like without the constant stream of traffic passing through the bottleneck created by their narrow main street.

In the course of his investigations, Telford found that there was still a toll on the Coldstream Bridge despite the fact that the intention of this had always been only to repay the capital costs; something which had been achieved many years before. Knowingly or otherwise, the travelling public and the residents of the town were being cheated. He recommended to a select committee that the tolls should cease immediately and that the surplus revenue from the bridge, with its interest, should be applied to secure the rebuilding of the bridge in the case of accident. His concern was the possibility of damage caused by *'the rapidity of the current in the river'*.

In the edition of The Kelso Mail of 16th January 1823 a full report is carried on a general meeting of a council held at Jedburgh the previous November. Its purpose was to consider the merits of the alternative ways to Newcastle; either by the existing one through Coldstream or the recent one through Jedburgh and over the Carter Fell. Naturally what Telford had to report on Coldstream Bridge was dealt with at some length and the following gives a flavour of the thoughts of members at the meeting:

> With regard to the Toll on Coldstream Bridge – the surplus revenue of which (as it is oddly termed) it is proposed to appropriate for the purpose of rebuilding the Bridge in the event of its destruction; – we have to observe that there is at this moment no legal Toll upon Coldstream Bridge; and that the Toll which has been, and still continues to be levied there, is an illegal extraction, which the Trustees have thought proper to enforce against the public. The Act of Parliament authorises a pontage upon Coldstream Bridge only until the debt upon it is paid. This debt has been extinguished for many years, as we learn from the Report before us; in which it is stated that a considerable surplus has been created - an accumulation which has obviously derived from an illegal Toll – extorted, among other things, upon every cartload of grain or coals passing over that bridge. We conceived this to be an object so immediately interesting to this County, as it affects its communication with Berwick and Northumberland'

The meeting finished without any immediate agreement on the favoured route but it was made quite clear that tolls on Coldstream Bridge had to cease. This probably led to protracted discussions with the Bridge Trustees, for it was not until 1826 that this was achieved. Unfortunately there appears to be no record of what happened to the surplus funds.

Coldstream Bridge c1900 showing the toll house. (from a postcard)

Tolls

Going south from Carfraemill, the first toll was about a mile along the road at Cleekhimin Bridge, then at Heckspathdean near Hexpath (later Houndslow), Castleloan east of Greenlaw, Springwells near Orange Lane, Fireburn Mill where the Kelso to Coldstream road joined and finally at Coldstream Bridge on the national boundary. This appears to be an excessive number of tolls for a road which is entirely within the borders of Berwickshire and it is likely that not all were in operation at the same time. Apart from Coldstream Bridge, by 1860 both Houndslow and Castleloan had been closed.

Coaching Inns

Coming from Edinburgh, there had been an inn at Huntershall but this had no facilities for horses. The first coaching inn was the New Channelkirk on the descent from Soutra, already referred to in Chapter 7.

The Carfraemill Inn probably dates from about the 1820s to replace those at New Channelkirk and Norton. Conveniently situated at the junction of the Coldstream road with the one to Lauder, it served for many years as a busy coaching inn, it being recorded that on one night no fewer than eighty horses were stabled there. In its time the inn has been considerably extended and modified and today it still flourishes under the recently-acquired title of 'The Lodge'.

Further down the road, another well-known inn was at Norton. Even at the start of the 19th century it was described as very old and may well have pre-dated coach traffic of any kind. It was on a road which no longer exists, that having been moved eastwards when the present road alignment was made to avoid Norton and the nearby Drummonds Hall (also an inn, but catering for the carrier trade rather than coaches). The lack of business at either establishment led to their closures. From the present roadway can be seen an old building with bricked-up windows and doors, thought to have been one of the main buildings of the Norton inn.

In the heyday of stagecoaches, several such services deviated from the Coldstream road to enter Lauder with its better facilities – these are dealt with in Chapter 9.

The next coaching inn was at Whiteburn, known as the Golden Eagle in 1808 and later simply as the Eagle. Long since closed, its business increased considerably when the new road to Kelso was opened in 1799. The main building still exists as a private house.

Towards Greenlaw, Tibby's Inn near Hexpath was a popular unofficial stop for some coaches. Horses were not changed there in coaching times, but might have been in the mid-18th century as it appeared in some of the early maps. All signs of Tibby's have now gone.

At Greenlaw, then the county town of Berwickshire, there was the Castle Inn which had been rebuilt in 1835 to serve the dual purpose as a coaching inn and for the councillors who used the new County Hall across the road. Although no stagecoaches passed this way after 1847 and Greenlaw lost its county town status to Duns in 1853, the inn continued and today is known as the Castle Inn Hotel.

Strangely perhaps in the circumstances, Coldstream never had anything other than some simple inns with no facilities for horses at any of them. Travellers had no option but to cross the border here for the short distance to Cornhill in Northumberland where there was an old coaching inn called the Beehive, its exact location in the village unknown. It went about the same time as the Collingwood Arms appeared in the early days of the 19th century. This interesting old inn is still in business and many visitors today are intrigued to find 'Post Horses' incised in the stonework above the door of the porch.

Chapter 9

The Edinburgh Roads to Jedburgh and Beyond (A68)

Map 8

Like the Great North Road, the old road from Edinburgh to Jedburgh was one of great antiquity although much less is known about it. It never shared the limelight because the primary purpose of the road (or rather trackway as it was then) was to provide communication between the Abbey in Jedburgh and Edinburgh, evidence for which appears in a 12th century charter. This is dealt with in chapter 3.

There appears to have been three roads south of Jedburgh which provided links with the road to Edinburgh. The oldest was Dere Street, which although passing Jedburgh two miles to the north-east, did give an easy way over the Cheviots from Rochester in Northumberland. Near the Roman camps at Pennymuir a track struck westwards through Middleknowes and Mossburnford then, avoiding the valley of the Jed Water, passed uphill from Fernihirst Castle and entered Jedburgh from the south-east. This is the way shown on Roy's 1750 map and also by Armstrong in his of 1777. Armstrong included a sketch map of the post roads between London and Edinburgh which showed *'a road along the Roman Watling Street'* from Catterick Bridge in Yorkshire, through Bishop Auckland and Hexham, on to Jedburgh then northwards to Edinburgh. At that time there was no reference whatsoever to the second road over the Cheviot Hills near Carter Fell from the head of historic Redesdale, although it had been used by armies and reivers as a quick means of getting in and out of English territory. From this, it must be assumed that the Roman road was still in extensive use in the middle of the 18th century, despite the steep gradients on the Cheviot section, particularly near Woden Law. It may have been this type of difficulty that led to the Carter Fell route becoming the preferred one.

The third road into Jedburgh from the south was the Wheel Causeway, already dealt with in Chapter 3. By the 18th century it was little used and probably sadly neglected.

These three routes would have converged at or near Jedburgh then made a common way northwards, probably following the general line of today's road through Newtown then on the recently-closed Bogle Burn road and into Melrose. Just west of there, near Darnick, the road joined another from Selkirk before crossing the

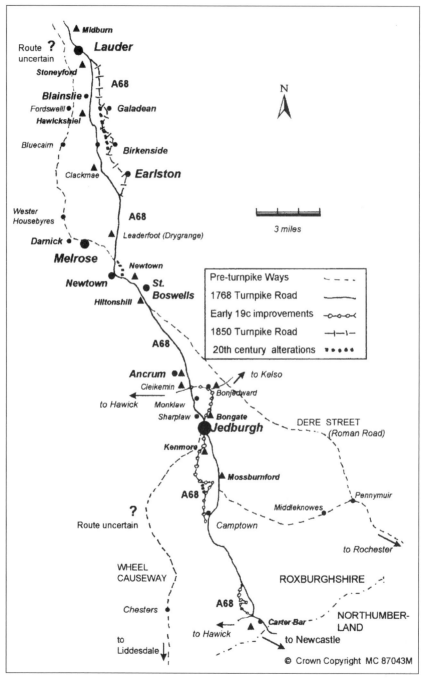

Map 8 – The Edinburgh Roads to Jedburgh and beyond.

Tweed. This is where a problem is encountered, for there were at least two crossing points within two miles of one another, both equidistant from the existing bridge at Lowood. The first was upstream and it was here we are told that there had been a very old wooden bridge from the early days of the Abbeys and that in 1544 it had been demolished by the English army as part of the general destruction of Melrose Abbey and associated property. The bridge did leave its name, however, for a small village known as Brigend grew up on the south bank and certainly the lands and town of Brigend or Bridgend are mentioned in a list of ecclesiastical properties in 1588.

For many years a ferry was used until a further bridge was built and from all accounts this was a very strange affair indeed. The ever-romantic Sir Walter Scott gives his own fanciful description of the bridge in his novel *The Monastery:*

A bridge of the very peculiar construction described in the text, actually existed at a small hamlet about a mile and a half above Melrose, called from the circumstance Bridge-end. It is thus noticed in Gordon's *Iter Septentrionale*:– "In another journey through the south parts of Scotland, about a mile and a half from Melrose in the shire of Teviotdale, I saw the remains of a curious bridge over the river Tweed, consisting of three octangular pillars, or rather towers, standing within the water, without any arches to join them. The middle one, which is the most entire, has a door towards the north, and I suppose, another opposite one towards the south, which I could not see without crossing the water. In the middle of this tower is a projection or cornice surrounding it; the whole is hollow from the door upwards, and now open at the top, near which was a small window. I was informed that not long ago a countryman and his family lived in this tower – and got his livelihood by laying out planks from pillar to pillar, and conveying passengers over the river. Whether this is ancient or modern, I know not; but as it is singular in its kind, I have thought fit to exhibit it."
The vestiges of this uncommon species of bridge still exist, and the author has often seen the foundations of the columns when drifting down the Tweed at night, for the purpose of killing salmon by torch-light. Mr. John Mercer of Bridge-end recollects, that about fifty years ago * the pillars were visible above water.'

*The Monastery first appeared in 1820, so this would have referred to a date around 1770.

Other accounts give the impression that there was a drawbridge which was lowered or lifted by means of a chain to achieve the same purpose. Milne, the Melrose historian writing in 1743 on the subject, referred to the old structure which had been washed away in a flood, leaving the ruined towers which were still standing in the waters. He went on: '...*there was a plain Way from this Bridge through the Muirs to Soutrahill, called yet the Girthgate*'. If this had been the crossing of the Girthgate (see chapter 3) then it was likely that the route would have followed today's road from Easter Langlee to Langshaw and Threepwood. From there the way now exists only as a footpath on the eastern side of the Allan Water but just before Lauder Common (about two miles west of Lauder) all trace of it has gone. To complicate matters, Armstrong in his 1771 map of Berwickshire clearly shows this way as proceeding on the west side of the stream then almost due north, making for Soutra Aisle.

The second crossing was downstream immediately north of Darnick and just west of Gattonside on the north bank. There had been a ford here since early times and Roy's Military Map of 1750 clearly shows a bridge here, with the inscription '*Road from Jedburgh to Lauder*' on the north side of the river. Only five years before there was no bridge over the Tweed anywhere in this area, for part of Prince Charlie's army had come this way and encountered some difficulty in crossing here. Jeffrey's History of Roxburghshire (1826) mentions a bridge at Cobblehaugh, a little above the rivulet of Darnick and next to it Salter's Ford '*which ran to the east of the Pavilion Cottage thence by Gattonside Bank, Easter Houses Byres through Mosshouses then Bluecairn and Blainslie*'. This mystery bridge disappeared by the time Stobie's Map of 1770 appeared, for on that one is shown the present bridge at Lowood.

Whatever way the route from Jedburgh might have taken across the Tweed, by the 18th century it then went due north on what is now part of the long-distance footpath known as The Southern Upland Way, through Bluecairn and Fordswell. There has been some disagreement about which way it went from there. One map of Roxburghshire dated about 1850 shows it making directly for Lauder, but some historians are of the opinion that instead of going into the town, it joined the Roman road on its way over the Lammermuir Hills to Soutra.

By the middle of that century it was becoming evident that the road was no longer suitable for the increasing amount of traffic using it, so that it became the subject of two early Turnpike Acts. The first was in 1760 to construct a new road over Soutra, details of which have already been dealt with in chapter 7 as regards that part north of Carfraemill. The second was in 1768 to provide what was essentially a new road between Lauder and the Tweed at Leaderfoot with considerable improvement to the existing one from Newtown to Jedburgh, then to England at Carter Fell.

From Carfraemill the road went down Lauderdale to Lauder, following very closely the actual route of today's highway. South of Lauder the new way went through Blainslie and Clackmae, passing within half a mile west of Earlston and then making for the Tweed at Leaderfoot. The way still exists as a series of minor unclassified roads serving local farms and communities. It is thought that for parts of its length, the line of Dere Street may have been followed which could help to account for the fact that few traces of the Roman road have ever been found on this stretch.

There had been a crossing of the Tweed at Leaderfoot (or Drygrange as it is sometimes called) by a ford and a ferry known as the 'Fly-boat' which indicates that this route had existed before the turnpike act. In 1780 a fine new bridge designed by Alexander Stevens was erected; with a central span of 115 feet it was regarded as quite exceptional for the period. Although today it is usually called the Drygrange Bridge, at first it was commonly referred to as the Fly Bridge; perhaps recalling the ferry's name. Like many of the bridges being built at that time, the designers could not have foreseen the amount or type of traffic which would use them in the future and this has led to their having to be replaced by wider but far less elegant structures to cope with today's volume of use. It is not known where the Romans crossed the Tweed from Trimontium; but with their knowledge it is quite possible that there was a bridge of a kind. It has been suggested that they would have found it very difficult to have coped with the steep north sides of the river at this point, indicating that they might have gone some way upstream to find a more gentle approach.

From the Tweed southwards the road followed the course of the present one, through Newtown and Lessudden (as St. Boswells village was called at that time) and along what is undoubtedly part of Dere Street. Just before Lilliardsedge, the new road diverged from the Roman one, taking a more westerly course but never very far from it. The Teviot was crossed by another fine structure built about 1782 and known as Ancrum Bridge although it is a mile from the village of that name. After the bridge the new turnpike crossed over the Hawick to Kelso road at Cleikemin, then, on a way no longer used as a public road, banked sharply to the left to avoid the steep gradients of the hill in Calderwood Woods. From there it followed the line of an existing rural road at Monklaw before passing Sharplaw and proceeding steeply into Jedburgh by way of Friars, now called Friarsgate.

South of Jedburgh, the old road on the east bank of the Jed Water was followed as far as Mossburnford, then a new way was made to Camptown where the Jed was joined by its tributary the Kaim Burn. It then took the high ground between these two waterways and appears to have climbed the steep hill to the ridge of the Cheviots known as Carter Fell. At 1371 feet, this is where it entered England and descended into Redesdale on its way to Newcastle.

It soon became apparent that the way south of Jedburgh, in particular the weary climb to Carter Fell with poor gradients, was not an ideal road for carriages. Early in the 19th century, the route was again changed, this time leaving Jedburgh immediately to the south and crossing the Jed Water three times within a mile to enable it to ascend the river valley by a much easier way on its west bank. It rejoined the former road at Camptown having made another (but last) crossing of the Jed. At about a mile from the summit, a new road veered off to the right of the old one and performed a short series of hairpin bends which enabled traffic to reach the top with far fewer problems.

The A68 road south of St. Boswells, looking towards the hazy Eildon Hills.

The remains of the Roman Road known as Dere Street, only a few yards from where the picture at the top was taken. The A68 and Dere Street run parallel to one another at this point.

In 1829 McAdam had been asked to make a report on this road and in it he submitted a plan for reducing the distance from Edinburgh to Newcastle by Jedburgh to 104 miles, 'the greater part of it level or nearly so – and no ascent upon the whole line exceeding an inclination of one foot in 25'. What is rather strange about this is that just a few years before, the distance by Jedburgh was calculated by Edward Mogg (a producer of reasonably accurate road-books) at 103 1/4 miles. In addition Thomas Telford had already reported on this road in 1823 in connection with the arguments surrounding the favoured route between the capitals. His survey revealed that the gradients on the Carter Fell section of the road only exceeded one in 25 on one stretch, this being one in 22 for a short distance.

McAdam proposed that the whole line from the Midlothian border at Caitha to the junction of the Ponteland Trust about 18 miles west of Newcastle should be consolidated in one trust. The cost of improvements was assessed at £25,000, a huge sum at that time, and this would have to be raised by borrowing on the credit of the tolls. There is no evidence that this interesting example of cross-border co-operation was ever achieved or even sought by the authorities concerned, but it does illustrate McAdam's keenness for trusts to work together to achieve maximum efficiency. This was obviously a problem he had already faced in other parts of the country.

This was the first reference to the possibility of the road from Edinburgh to Jedburgh being altered so that it would run along the Gala valley to Galashiels before going through Melrose to join the original way from Lauder at Newtown. At that time, coaches to Jedburgh were already coming that way, so benefiting from passing through many more places than by way of Lauderdale.

Whether by the influence of Telford or McAdam, it appears that around the second decade of the century the finishing touches were put on the more difficult aspects of the road of the Cheviot Hills and in 1830 the first scheduled coaches ran on it. The road became very popular with travellers who found the way shorter than by Berwick or Coldstream.

Other improvements made by the Trustees from the early part of the 19th century were to the north of Jedburgh. Instead of the road at Cleikemin going south straight over the hill as before, it now turned to join the Hawick to Kelso road until Bonjedward, then followed an improved Kelso to Jedburgh road close to the Jed Water and into the town.

It was not until the 1850s that a completely new road between Lauder and Newtown by way of Earlston had been planned, using part of a turnpike created for the Kelso road twenty years before. Instead of going through Blainslie, it now turned south-eastwards at Stoneyford Toll and proceeded to follow the Leader Water on its west bank until it was crossed at Galadean close to the existing bridge on the Kelso road. From Birkenside it proceeded to Earlston on the already-established Kelso road, from where a short new section was made southwards to meet the first turnpike coming in from the west side on its way to Leaderfoot.

These alterations came late in the history of turnpike trusts and were probably the last major road improvements anywhere in the Borders prior to county councils taking over responsibility later in the century.

With the large increase in traffic during this century this road became a very busy one, especially after local rail services disappeared in the 1960s. The A68 is now a major route from Yorkshire into Scotland over the moors, through some splendid countryside which makes it a favoured way by many tourists. For many people south of the border, the dramatic view from Carter Bar is an admirable first sight of Scotland.

Much of the way has been widened and improved, notably around Lauder, where the Roman-like straightness leads to much speeding by motorists. At two places, Galadean and near Mossburnford south of Jedburgh, loops on the road have been cut across, so slightly shortening the distance. At least three of the bridges have had to be entirely rebuilt; at Galadean, Leaderfoot (Drygrange) and Ancrum, although fortunately the old ones have been preserved. It is interesting to compare the old with the new; the box-girder bridge of 1973 at Leaderfoot, for example, may be very functional but it lacks all the grace of the old one or the majesty of the nearby railway viaduct, the three irreverently collectively referred to as Tripontium. The old bridge at Ancrum was one of the first to be replaced, being done as early as 1940. South of Jedburgh, the numerous bridges there were all rebuilt this century, in a somewhat severe style.

Coaching Inns

The inns at New Channelkirk and Carfraemill have already been mentioned. South of there the first inn was at Lauder, the famous Black Bull which in its time was probably one of the busiest of all the Border inns. At its height it served two daily London coaches in either direction as well as local services to Jedburgh, Kelso and Duns. This building had been a coaching inn since the earliest days and it was enlarged to its present state early in the 19th century to cope with the increased amount of traffic. The Eagle Inn is also referred to as a coaching inn, but it does not appear to have attracted custom from the coach operators, relying perhaps more on the private carriage trade. Both inns are still in business today.

Leaderfoot Bridge, on the Edinburgh to Jedburgh road, looking north about 1905. Apart from the telegraph poles, the scene as depicted here is probably little changed from the time the bridge was built in 1780. (from a postcard)

The same bridge today, but now out of use, having been superseded (and overwhelmed) by the concrete structure erected in 1973.

The next coaching inn was the Salmon at Drygrange Bridge about which very little is known. It ceased to exist in the 1820s, probably a victim of the decision to run the coach from Edinburgh to Jedburgh down the Gala Valley instead of Lauderdale.

The Spread Eagle Hotel in Jedburgh, the terminus of the Edinburgh stagecoach services and a stopping point for the London coaches.

The last stop in Scotland was at Jedburgh. In the early days of the stagecoach, the last inn and staging-post was here in the form of the Black Bull in the Canongate, but later it was transferred to the Spread Eagle in the High Street, another favourite with travellers and still there today. From Jedburgh, it was a long haul to the Carter Bar and although there had been an inn near the top it had no facilities for horses. They were expected to last out for another six miles until Byrness Inn was reached.

Tolls

A formidable number of tolls were erected on this route: south of Soutra the first was at Midburn, north of Lauder, then at Stoneyford (south of the town close to the entry into Roxburghshire), Hawickshiel at Blainslie, Clackmae near Earlston, Drygrange Bridge, Newtown, Hiltonshill (south of St. Boswells), Ancrum and Monteviot side-bars (within a few yards of one another), Cleikemin, Jedburgh (Bongate) and Jedburgh (Kenmore) which was just to the south of the ancient bridge there. Finally there was the famous border toll at Carter Fell which gave rise to the name of the pass today, Carter Bar. It was not actually on the border-line, but at the nearby junction with the Hawick road. Like a number of other tolls it had also been an inn at one time.

Until the road south of Jedburgh was moved to the west bank, there had been a toll at Mossburnford. When the new road south of Lauder was constructed in the 1850s, the Hawickshiel and Clackmae tolls were closed. As the demise of the toll system was by then becoming apparent, no new tolls were ever built on the new road through Earlston. When the final stage of the road before Jedburgh was completed, Cleikemin was also closed, to be replaced by Bonjedward.

Chapter 10

The Edinburgh Roads to Kelso (A68, A697, A6089, B6397)

Map 9

A way to Kelso may have come into existence in the 12th century when Edinburgh replaced Dunfermline as the Scottish capital. It would then have become necessary to establish communications between the new capital and the Royal Burgh of Roxburgh, as well as the nearby abbey at Kelso just across the Tweed. Roxburgh then was one of the most important of Scottish towns, ranking with Stirling and Berwick and even boasting a mint at one time, but all trace of it has now gone. It lay to the west of Kelso on a strategic site; the Tweed formed an arc round it on the west, north and east sides with the Teviot fulfilling the same function to the south. Behind it lay Roxburgh Castle on an imposing mound, of which nothing more than a few crumbling pieces of masonry have survived. Somewhere along the Tweed near Roxburgh there had been a stone bridge in the 14th century but, like the town, all traces have now gone.

Travellers from Kelso Abbey and the town of Roxburgh probably made their way north-westwards to Dere Street, then the only permanent trackway to the north. Later, and certainly from the 16th century, a more definite way was in use. This left Kelso through the grounds of what are now the policies of Floors Castle, then passed the village of Smailholm to continue in a north-westerly direction through the hamlets of Legerwood and Boon. Near the latter the Boondreigh Water was crossed by a ford (one of the few of any size on this way) before joining the Coldstream road at High Cross, then continuing on to join Dere Street. At that time High Cross was an important meeting of the ways; north to Edinburgh, west to Lauder, south to Kelso and east to Coldstream, and today these survive other than the one from Kelso which is now no more than a rough track marking the way to Boon.

This road remained in use until the middle of the 18th century, but by that time it was apparent that if carriages were to be used, some radical improvements would have to be made. The necessary Turnpike Act for this was passed in 1765, authorising the building of a largely new road from Lauder to Kelso and extending it to the March Burn on the Northumberland border . The latter part will be dealt with in chapter 16.

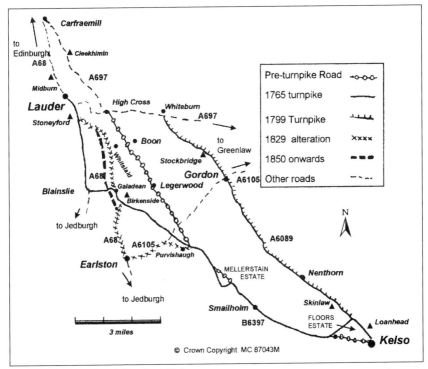

Map 9 – The Edinburgh Roads to Kelso.

In Chapter 7 it was shown that an earlier Act had set up the new road over the Lammermuirs at Soutra. South of Lauder the road proceeded in a south-easterly direction through Blainslie, from where, two years later, another new road would be continued southwards towards Jedburgh. The Kelso road then turned eastwards to cross the Leader Water at a fine new bridge at Galadean. Close by at Birkenside, the road left the valley and went over a lonely moor, still going south-eastwards to join with the ancient way which had come through Legerwood. At Mellerstain, instead of taking the old direct way, the road had to be deviated to avoid the policies of the recently-completed estate, which meant two right-angle bends within a few hundred yards of one another which still exist today. Thereafter, the road followed the line of the old one until two miles before Kelso. Here, just as at Mellerstain, a new estate had been created and as the Duke of Roxburghe had no need for a public road passing so close to his fine new mansion at Floors, so the way was once more deviated, actually going north-eastwards, then south-eastwards, before entering Kelso on a new road outside the Duke's estate but at a point close by the main gateway to it. From there it went down what is now Roxburgh Street to the Square in the centre of the town.

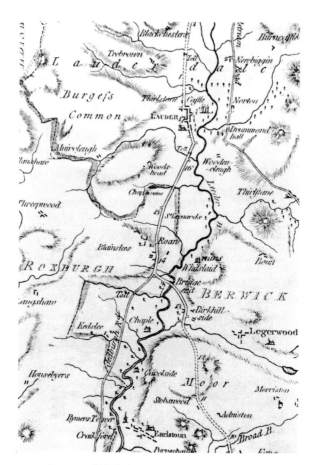

Part of the post road survey of M. J. Armstrong in 1776 showing the countryside south of Lauder with the Jedburgh road following the west side of the Leader Water. The Kelso road leaves it at Blainlees (Blainslie) and passes Birkenside before crossing the moor. Note that at that time no road served Earlston (seen at the foot of the map).

This was the first road capable of taking carriages from Edinburgh to Kelso in most weather conditions. The earliest coaches to Kelso used this route, but it was not popular as some of the gradients were quite severe. Inevitably, there were demands for further improvements but it was not until 1799 that a further Turnpike Act was passed to create an entirely new way to Kelso, this time by a route further to the east. It started at Whiteburn Inn on the Coldstream road, crossed through a sparsely populated area of moorland and on to the village of Gordon, or West Gordon as it was known then. Skirting the east side of the Mellerstain estate, the road then went though Nenthorn where another fine bridge had been constructed to take the road over the Eden Water. This bridge is still in use today, despite being far too narrow to handle modern traffic. From there it was a straightforward downhill journey into Kelso, meeting the other road through Smailholm at the corner of the Floors estate. Today this road remains the principal one between the capital and Kelso.

The other road by Birkenside and Smailholm continued to be used until 1829 when it was partially replaced by a further new road which started just south of Lauder. It crossed the Leader Water by a new bridge to Whitslaid, then on to Galadean to rejoin the old road. At Birkenside the roads diverged again, this time the new one continuing to follow the valley of the Leader to Earlston, the first time this town had ever been connected by a turnpike road. It then turned eastwards through Purvishaugh before once again rejoining the old road and on to Kelso as before. The way over the moors from Birkenside was no longer used by coach traffic and although it remained as a public road until well into this century, it now survives only as a farm track.

When the new road to Jedburgh south of Lauder was built in the 1850s, then this also took the Kelso traffic as far as Earlston and the 1829 route by Whitslaid was closed. The modern alterations made to that part of the route have already been referred to in chapter 9.

Coaching Inns

The inns in the north have already been dealt with in chapters 7 and 9. After Lauder there were no more until Kelso was reached, although horses were sometimes changed at an ale-house at Smailholm. In Kelso however it was a very different matter.

The first bridge over the Tweed at Kelso, built in 1754 and destroyed by flood in 1797. (from an engraving)

People in Kelso saw the opportunity for their town to take full advantage of the coach industry and the Cross Keys Inn was built in the Market Square about 1769, perhaps at that time the best of all the Border facilities for travellers. It replaced an earlier inn of the same name close by when plans were being made for stagecoaches through the town and it was anticipated that London coaches may well go that way. This did happen but not for many years later.

The White Swan Inn, Kelso, as it might have been early in the 19th century before its demolition to make way for a bank. (from a drawing made in the 1930s by an unknown artist)

Earlier, in 1754 the Kelso bridge over the Tweed had been constructed in place of the ford and ferry which had existed previously and it was thought that this too would also be an inducement for long-distance coaches to go that way instead of the difficult journey on the Great North Road. A toll road had been constructed through Kelso to connect with Wooler in Northumberland, but it never proved popular with coaches and no established services ever went that way. It could not compete in popularity with the road by Coldstream following the completion of the bridge there in 1766, for this way had become the preferred route into England and the one selected for the first properly-established stagecoach route between Edinburgh and London in 1785. To the disappointment of the Kelso traders, it went by Greenlaw, not Kelso.

Prior to 1800, the only evidence of a coach through the town was in 1771 when a notice in the *Edinburgh Advertiser* that the 'Flying Post' was to run between Edinburgh and Newcastle. On its return journey to Edinburgh, passengers would spend a night in Kelso. Unfortunately there appears to be no other reference to this service or anything like it at that date and one is left wondering if, in fact, it ever managed to run at all.

Three other coaching inns were the Queen's Head in Bridge Street, the White Swan in the Market Place and the King's Arms in Roxburgh Street. Of these the Queens Head continues to trade at the same premises, but the White Swan had to move to a new building in Abbey Row when their original building was demolished to make way for the building of the Commercial Bank early in the 19th century. The King's Arms Inn has completely disappeared.

The proprietors of the Cross Keys and White Swan inns were the first in the town to operate stagecoaches, running their services to Edinburgh and later to other places in competition with one another.

Tolls

The tolls on the first road were at Stoneyford (south of Lauder), Birkenside, then Loanhead on the approaches to Kelso. Birkenside was closed after the new road through Earlston was opened. The other road through Gordon produced tolls at Stockbridge near the Legerwood turnoff and at Skinlaw about two miles north of Kelso.

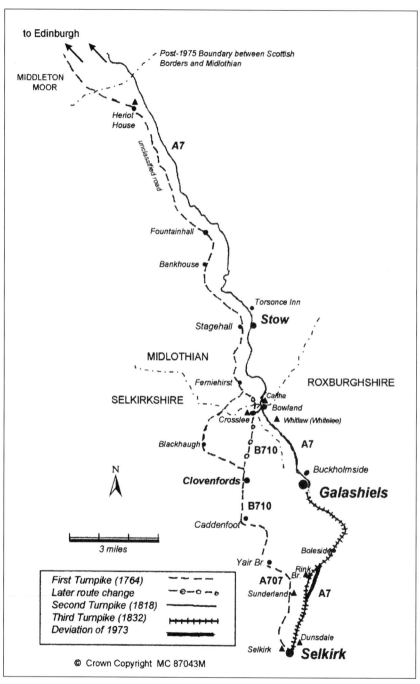

Map 10 – The Edinburgh Roads to Selkirk.

Chapter 11

The Edinburgh Roads to Carlisle through Selkirk and Hawick (A7)

Maps 10 and 11

Prior to the Union of the Crowns in 1603, it is unlikely that much use would have been made of any kind of road between north-west England and Edinburgh. Until then it was the reivers who did most of the travelling and they did not need roads to get about; they could find their way over the Border hills day and night in any kind of weather. The importance of this road then was not so much its southern destination, but the fact that it went through two old Border towns, Selkirk and Hawick.

For convenience, the road south from Edinburgh has been arbitrarily divided at Selkirk.

Edinburgh to Selkirk – Map 10

Like so many of the other Border routes, Dere Street was the original way over the Lammermuirs, then the Jedburgh road mentioned in Chapter 9 to the Tweed crossing near Darnick. From there the road followed the Tweed and its tributary the Ettrick, passing by the ruins of Lindean Kirk before arriving at Selkirk by the north-east. In Ainslie's 1773 map of Selkirkshire, this way was shown as 'the road to Melrose'.

It was the Gala valley (or Wedale to use its medieval name) which was selected to take the first turnpike road from Edinburgh to Selkirk when the requisite parliamentary act was obtained in 1764. But before then, it appears some people were already using the Gala valley to go to Edinburgh from Selkirk and there is the often-related story of the Selkirk carrier who took his wagon and horses along the bed of the river in the drier weather as a better alternative to what passed for a road.

Later destined to become an important industrial Border town, Galashiels was then still no more than a village, so unimportant indeed that no thought was given to this turnpike going through it.

South from Edinburgh, a number of ways seem to have been used, but the main one went by Liberton Kirk, Lasswade, Dalhousie and Middleton, all in Midlothian or Edinburghshire as it then was. The way south of Middleton went over the moor of the same name then crossed a ridge of the Moorfoot Hills to Heriot House on the headwaters of the Gala Water. From there the road followed the west bank of the Gala Water through Fountainhall, Bankhouse and on to Stagehall, opposite the village of Stow. A few miles further on, south of Ferniehirst Farm, it bore away from the river and went uphill until it reached the Caddon Water near Blackhaugh. It then followed the Caddon through Clovenfords to join the Tweed at Caddonfoot. There it ran by the left bank until Fairnilee Farm was reached and here the river was crossed on a fine new three-arched bridge. Called the Yair Bridge after the adjoining house of the same name, this handsome structure still carries traffic on the road between Peebles and Selkirk. From there the road passed High Sunderland before crossing Selkirk Bridge and into the town.

The Yair Bridge over the Tweed at Fairnilee, built in 1760 to carry the first turnpike road between Edinburgh and Selkirk. A building close by looks remarkably like a toll house, but there are no references to it in Trustee records.

Soon after the new turnpike road came into use, another route was made after Ferniehirst Farm. Instead of leaving the river valley, this road continued to follow the Gala as far as Crosslee and from there it went by a new way to Clovenfords, then as before on to Yair Bridge and Selkirk. This effectively cut the long detour by the Caddon Water. The first route was probably an existing track which the turnpike trustees decided to improve until the new section could be built.

This 1764 road to Selkirk was most unpopular with travellers, for it went through some wild countryside with few facilities. Several stretches were so poor that the road was frequently lost under a sea of mud; this being especially true of the section which crossed Middleton Moor. But it had been a considerable improvement on what had passed for a track before that. Mrs. Russell from Ashiestiel gave a fascinating account of a family's ride to Edinburgh in the days immediately prior to the turnpike road. They had ridden up the Gala valley, crossing and recrossing the river many times. When the track turned to the left to go over Middleton Moor, so avoiding the deep deans between Borthwick and Crichton, they found that the way was completely unmarked and quite treacherous. The new road, for all its failings, must have been a boon to people like them.

In the late years of the 18th century, when coaches were beginning to become a popular means of travel, local trustees were being urged to build an entirely new road up the Gala valley. Because of its favourable siting for watermills, Galashiels was growing rapidly as a textile manufacturing centre, but it suffered from the handicap of having no turnpike roads to serve it. The heaviest pressure however came from the Post Office, who were so unimpressed with the existing road that they threatened to withdraw direct mail services from Selkirk and Hawick to Edinburgh, so leaving these places with only a link through Kelso to Berwick. This would not only have caused unnecessary delays but also meant that postal charges would cost a lot more, for in those days letters were charged by the distance actually travelled.

The Post Office particularly grudged the long rides through what they referred to as the 'dreary and uninhabited country' between Selkirk and Edinburgh. The postal service was withdrawn for a while in 1804, but the quick intervention of the Duke of Buccleuch soon brought it back again and by 1807, a full mailcoach service between Edinburgh and Carlisle was in operation, despite the lack of progress on a replacement road.

But plans were afoot for an entirely new road along the opposite bank of the Gala Water, one which would avoid the worst of Middleton Moor by striking out on a new line further east. Like the road it would replace, it had to run quite close to the river as the land in the valley rises quite steeply on both sides. Throughout the valley the river winds its way tortuously through the narrow flat bed and this is why both roads have very few straight sections. Even today, it is not an easy journey, the way being cursed with numerous difficult bends. When the railway was built along the same valley in 1849, this difficulty was overcome by building no fewer than fourteen rail bridges over the river before Galashiels was reached.

Like most other roads at the time, it was built over a period and appears to have been completed and opened in full for traffic in 1818. It went through Stow for the first time, where the event was celebrated with the building of the Torsonce Inn a quarter of a mile north of the village. At the same time, Stow acquired a post office when the one at Stagehall across the river was closed. Further south, a new bridge had already been built in 1815 to cross the Gala Water at Bowland to connect with Crosslee. After this was crossed the road met the existing one on its way to Clovenfords and on to Selkirk. From Bowland, the road was extended along the river through Buckholmside to create the first carriage road to connect Galashiels with the capital. In the same year a new bridge was built over the Gala Water in the town to replace the dangerous old one. This in turn was replaced in 1889 and although much altered, it is still in use today. This new road north of Galashiels is essentially today's A7.

Unlike in England, the activities of highwaymen north of the border were few and far between, mainly because of the great patience which would have had to have been exercised by them when waiting for the next victim to come along the deserted Scottish roads. As far as can be found, the only instances of highwaymen in the Borders occurred along the stretch of road between Bowland and Galashiels. In 1827 Robert Aimers from Galashiels was attacked and robbed on it whilst passing Buckholm Wood. Two weeks later a Mr Ingram was attacked on his horse but when his servant caught up with him, the highwayman fled. A few nights later, Robert Howden was knocked senseless and robbed. The robber or robbers were never captured. None of these incidents involved persons travelling by coach.

The last link in the chain of this highway was completed with great ceremony in 1832. This took the route south-eastwards from Galashiels, past Boleside on the banks of the Tweed and over two new bridges, both constructed by the Darnick builders John and Thomas Smith at a cost of £2500. The first was over the Tweed and known as the Rink Bridge after the nearby house of the same name, or sometimes more simply (but confusingly) as the Tweed Bridge. The second was close by, over the Ettrick Water and was also known by two names, either Lindean Bridge after the nearby village or Ettrick Bridge. From these bridges an entirely new road was built into the town centre of Selkirk. Before this section was built, there had been a road of sorts from Selkirk to Galashiels but it was a dangerous one, especially for carriages, with travellers from time to time falling foul of the fords which had to be negotiated. This effectively completed the last link in the turnpike system between Edinburgh and Selkirk, creating a highway that enabled stagecoach operators to maximise their services.

This road remained in this format until 1973 when it was decided that it could be re-aligned by taking advantage of the disused railway line south of Galashiels, creating a new Tweed crossing on the site of the railway bridge there. This meant

The Rink Bridge (1832) over the Tweed near its confluence with the Ettrick Water (on the lower left of the picture). This bridge carried the busy A7 traffic north of Selkirk until the new bridge was completed in 1973. This picture was taken from the new bridge.

that the two fine 1832 bridges, somewhat narrow to cope with modern traffic, were now redundant. Fortunately they still stand as monuments to local craftsmanship.

Coaching Inns

The Queen's Head Inn at Bankhouse was on the first turnpike road and this was used by the early stagecoach operators as a staging-post. Mailcoaches stopped at Stagehall opposite Stow where there had been a post office which served Galashiels, amongst other places, until they had their own in 1803. The Clovenfords Inn, which dates from the mid-1700s, seems to have had no regular provision for changing horses, but it was a convenient stopping-place for coaches. It closed in 1818 when the coaches started to go by the new road through Galashiels but reopened later that century and today remains in business.

With the completion of the road on the east bank of the Gala Water, the Queen's Head was closed and in its place an entirely new inn was built in 1819 to the north of Stow. Somewhat confusingly it was called The Torsonce Inn, although the house of the same name lies a mile south of the village. The reason for this was that the inn had been built by the Cockham Burn on the mill lands owned by the Torsonce estate. According to the Rev. David Weddell, minister of Stow, the inn was *'much admired by travellers as perhaps unequalled in any country inn in Scotland'*. It was built by subscription by seven heritors in the county of Edinburgh and eight in Selkirkshire and Roxburghshire at a cost of £2884 to complete. It is not known exactly when it closed, but was probably quite soon after the arrival of the railway through Stow to Galashiels in 1849.

When the last part of the new road was completed to Selkirk in 1832, stagecoaches started to pass through the centre of Galashiels for the first time and the Bridge Inn was built to cater for this trade, although it does not appear that many, if any, horse changes were made there. The basic purpose of the inn seems to have been for picking up and setting down passengers.

In Selkirk, the original coaching inn was The Cross Keys in Market Place, but this was replaced before 1830 by the purpose-built Grapes Inn in the High Street, later to have its name changed to The County Hotel. It is still there today, but all the stables at the rear have been demolished. Confusingly, there is a Cross Keys Hotel today in Market Place but it is on the other side of the road from the original and there appears to have been no business connection between them.

Tolls

Toll-gates were built along both roads; on the old one at Heriot House in Midlothian, Crosslee just after the Selkirkshire boundary had been crossed, Sunderland (near the farm of the same name) and then on to one at Selkirk. This was not in the town itself, but on the other side of the Ettrick Water near Linglie Farm. In its time, Sunderland Toll had acquired at least two name variations, High Sunderland and Sunderland Hall and the first toll had been slightly further north at a bridge over the Howdenpol Burn.

With the completion of the new road, tolls were built at Caitha on the Midlothian side of the county boundary, then nearby at Whitelee (sometimes referred to as Whitlaw) as the road enters Roxburghshire. These were followed by ones at the Rink Bridge (known as 'The Pontage Toll') and at Dunsdale on the northern approaches to Selkirk. This replaced the Shawburn toll on the old road to Melrose which was closed when the new road opened in 1832. Traditionally the three tolls at Selkirk, Sunderland and Shawburn (later Dunsdale) were let to one tenant and when the new road arrived, it was necessary for compensation to be paid for the reduction in business at the first two.

Selkirk to Carlisle – Map 11

The old road south of Selkirk more or less followed the existing A7 as far as Ashkirk, but within a mile after there, it deviated to the west and went over Drinkstone Hill on a track which can still be seen there. Then it continued by what

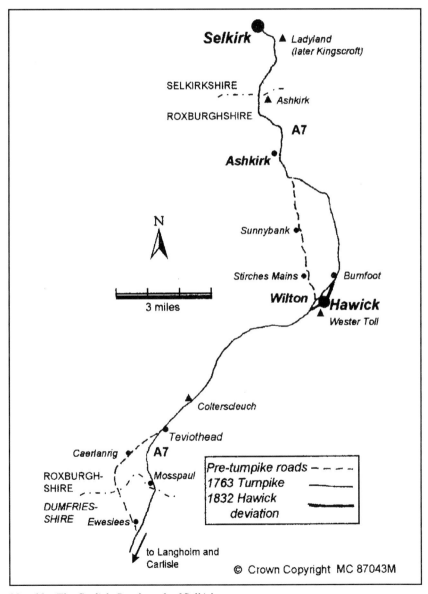

Map 11 – The Carlisle Road south of Selkirk.

are now farm roads through Sunnybank and passing by Stirches Mains on its way to Wilton and Hawick.

From Hawick to the Dumfriesshire border, most of the old road followed the same way as now but there appears to have been a deviation after Teviothead, for an old road turned to the right there and past the farm of Caerlanrig, proceeding up the valley of the Limiecleuch Burn, before rejoining the existing road at Eweslees. It is not clear whether this was the only way before the turnpike road was made or whether it was an alternative, but evidence has been found of wheeled traffic on this road and indeed the term 'coach road' had been used locally to describe it. It is hard to imagine what sort of coach traffic would have used that road before the middle of the 18th century – it must have been a very rare occurrence.

The Turnpike Act of 1763 led to the creation of the road known today, most of it new south of Ashkirk. It took a more easterly route a few miles from the original way and entered into the Teviot valley at what is now called Burnfoot to proceed through the village of Wilton and cross the river to enter Hawick. It was not until 1832 that the North Bridge was constructed further downstream, so enabling a more direct approach to the town avoiding Wilton.

From Hawick the road southwards was more or less the same as today's highway, allowing for a small deviation or two following road improvements over the years. At Mosspaul the county boundary was crossed and from there the road went, as it had done for years, through Langholm, crossing the national border into England, passing Longtown and into Carlisle.

No major route changes have been made in modern times, but south of Selkirk on the way to Hawick much widening and straightening out has taken place, with cuttings and embankments, to create a very fine stretch of highway. Through the moor-lands south of Hawick, there appears to be constant road-works as lengths of the road are gradually improved.

Coaching Inns

The only coaching inns on this stretch were at Hawick and Mosspaul. In the early days, facilities at Hawick were not very good, for according to a traveller in 1800 *'I would advise you to get early to Hawick, lest other travellers should be there before you; there is but one sitting room at Hawick and only one tolerable bed-chamber, with two beds in it'*. It is not known which property was being referred to, but at that time the Tower Inn was the usual posting-house. This was a 15th century building put to many different uses in its time, but made into a coaching-inn about 1773.

The exhausting pull up to the Mosspaul Inn (which stands just over 800 feet high on the Dumfriesshire border) necessitated extra horses, but when the inn was built in 1800, there was no stabling because, it was said, horses could not be kept at that altitude! So travellers had to be content with refreshments. Fortunately, provision for horses was made later and the inn became known as one of the most picturesque and eagerly-anticipated rest houses on the Carlisle road. It remains a popular stopping place today.

Outside the Borders, there were further coaching inns at Langholm (The George) and at Longtown (Graham's Arms) with a choice of the Bush or its rival The Coffee House in Carlisle. These Carlisle hostelries were famous and in the 1820s between them they saw off eleven stagecoaches and seven mailcoaches each day.

Tolls

On the turnpike road south of Selkirk, the first toll was just out of the town at Ladyland. In the 1830s when the new road to Kelso was completed, a toll known as Kingscroft was built at its intersection with the one to Hawick, within a short distance of Ladyland. It was not long before the latter was closed with Kingscroft toll having the dual function of serving both roads. Confusingly, both names were used afterwards, although the Trustee minutes seemed to favour Ladyland.

The next was where the road crossed into Roxburghshire, referred to as Ashkirk although it was about two miles north of that village. In Hawick, the Wester Toll was in Buccleuch Street. The last toll in Roxburghshire was at Colterscleuch, just to the north of Teviothead. The obvious place for this would have been at Mosspaul, but perhaps they thought that tollkeepers, like horses, could not survive at that height.

Chapter 12

The Edinburgh Roads to Moffat (A701)

Map 12, A and B

This was the most important road in Peeblesshire in the 18th century, for it took the well-heeled citizens of Edinburgh to Moffat in Dumfriesshire to 'partake of the waters' there. A sulphur spring had been discovered in Moffat in 1630 and its reputation as a spa soon grew, making it one of the most accessible to the élite of the capital. It was for this reason that no fewer than three inns appeared in the sparsely populated area of Tweedsmuir, only one of which, the Crook Inn, survives today.

Prior to the improvements made following the turnpiking of the road, it ran from Edinburgh, sharing the Biggar road as far as where Carlops stands now. It then turned southwards to Linton (now West Linton) and carried on in the same general direction towards Blyth Bridge. There the road joined with another route from Edinburgh via Howgate which had entered the county at Leadburn and continued through Noblehouse and Romanno Bridge following the exact line of the present A701. Both these routes were in use but it appears that when coaches came on the scene, the way through West Linton was the favoured one, or perhaps more accurately, the lesser of two evils. The state of both roads was a constant source of complaints.

From Blyth Bridge the road continued to Broughton, passing to the eastern side of the infamous Mount Bog, regarded as the most dangerous part of the road in all but perfect weather. Just south of Broughton, the Tweed valley was met and this was followed to the source of the river close to the Dumfriesshire border.

The clamour for better roads led to the Turnpike Act of 1753, which in addition to the Biggar road already mentioned, also applied to both branches of the route, referred to at the time as the Linton and Noblehouse roads. For most of the way there were few radical changes, but two of note should be mentioned. First an entirely new way over the Dumfriesshire border was created to get better gradients for coach traffic and secondly the moving of the road at Mount Bog to the west of the obstruction, where it remains to this day. Otherwise the work was mainly remedial, with new foundations and better drainage. Writing in the First Statistical Account 1793/99, the minister at Broughton said that the main road was in good repair *'but the bye-roads are very bad'*. At Tweedsmuir however, it was reported that the main road was often in a bad state, *'but will now meet with thorough repair'*.

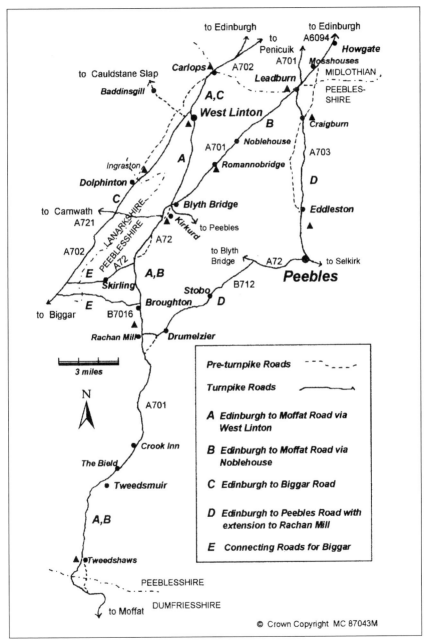

Map 12 – The Edinburgh Roads to Moffat, Peebles and Biggar.

Early in the 19th century, the Linton road was gradually losing favour with both the general public and the Post Office, the latter being one of the principal users since the inauguration of the mailcoach service between Edinburgh and Dumfries in 1806. By 1833 it had been decided to make no further use of the road between West Linton and Blyth Bridge for coach traffic, so that everything of importance now went by way of Leadburn and Noblehouse. It gradually fell into disrepair and although the first half to the south of West Linton remains in use today as a public road, the second part to Blyth Bridge is now no more than farm-tracks.

About the same time, the settlement of Kirkurd south of Blyth Bridge was by-passed to the west. Today this road, the A701, is the main route between Edinburgh and Dumfries via Moffat, but it rarely appears to be a very busy one.

Extract from one of the well-known strip maps by Taylor & Skinner (1776) showing the roads around Kirkurd in Peeblesshire at that time. (Note that this map is upside down in that south is at the top). Most of the roads shown have been considerably altered since then.

Coaching Inns

On the original road, the Raemartin was the coaching inn in the centre of West Linton, built in 1789 and still there today. When the way was changed to go by Leadburn, the Leadburn Inn there was already well established, having been founded in 1777 to cater for the army of drovers passing that way with their black Highland cattle. It was provident for the owners that just as the droving trade was diminishing, so along came the profitable coaches to make up for it. Even when the railways supplanted the coaches, they took advantage of this too by converting it into a railway hotel.

At different times, coaches stopped at a variety of small inns on the road southward, at places such as Noblehouse, Romanno Bridge, Blyth Bridge and Broughton, but little about them is known or whether any of them had facilities for changing horses.

The Crook Inn in Tweedsmuir, reputedly one of the oldest licensed premises inScotland. Much altered in the 1930s.

The next coaching inn was well known. The Crook Inn in Tweedsmuir, is reputedly one of the oldest licensed premises in Scotland. Licences were first issued in 1604, so it is quite likely that it was even older than that. The history of this famous inn is an exciting one with stories of Covenanters, daring escapes and involvement of one of the owners in the battle at Culloden. The original building is still there, but now unrecognisable because of heavy alterations carried out in the characteristic but somewhat charmless style of the 1930s. This is one of the few truly country inns in the Borders to have survived the end of the coaching era.

Just over a mile further up the valley of the Tweed was The Bield (sometimes Beild) built in 1726 at a time when the spa at Moffat was enjoying popularity with Edinburgh folk. There appears to have been much competition with the Crook Inn down the road, but of the two Robert Burns preferred the Bield. It also contained the post office for Tweedsmuir from 1765 until 1813, when it passed to the Crook. In 1821 a further building was added to the original and confusingly the stone carrying the date 1726 was moved over to it. Unlike its neighbour it did not survive as an inn and today it is a private house, but the courtyard for the coaches is still there. An old saying in the Borders is to give the extent of the Tweed valley as being 'from Berwick to The Bield', so at least the name was perpetuated in this way.

The third coaching inn was at Tweedshaws much further up the road and almost at the Dumfriesshire border. It too did not survive. This inn saw the final act of one of the worst tragedies to befall coach travel. In 1831, the northbound mailcoach was overcome by a blizzard north of Moffat near the natural depression known since reiving times as the Devil's Beef Tub. After seeing that the passengers were safely taken back to Moffat, the driver and the guard then set out on foot through the thick snow with the bags of the mail which, according to the Post Office rules, 'had to get through'. It cost them their lives in the atrocious conditions and ironically when their bodies were found the next morning, each clutching a precious mailbag, they were lying within a short distance of the safety of the inn. Today their brave effort to get the mail through is commemorated in a monument by the side of the road.

Tolls

There were tolls at Carlops and West Linton on the old road and when the route was changed, others at Leadburn and Romanno Bridge were used. The latter was already well established, for it handled much of the cattle traffic on the drove road from Cauldstane Slap, indeed half of its income came from that source. Until the road through Kirkurd was moved westwards, there had been a toll there by the same name. The one at Harestanes was then shared with traffic using the cross-route from Glasgow to Peebles. Further south there were tolls at Rachan Mill and at Tweedshaws within a mile of the border with Dumfriesshire.

Chapter 13

The Edinburgh Roads to Peebles (A703)

Map 12, D

According to George Pringle in his *Counties of Peebles and Selkirk*, the original road to Edinburgh from Peebles did not take the direct way to the north of the town, but left much further west past Jedderfield (presumably following the old Roman road at that stage) before turning northwards to reach Eddleston. He went on to say that this was the case until 1770 when the present road was built. However Edgar's 1741 map of Peeblesshire clearly shows today's road, so it is quite likely that it is much older than he thought.

Today's road from Edinburgh leaves the A701 Moffat road at Leadburn and follows closely the course of the Eddleston Water southwards to Peebles, the only village on the way being Eddleston itself. Originally, the road took a different course through the northern part of the valley. It did not start at Leadburn but near Mosshouses, about a mile nearer Edinburgh, crossing over today's road at Craigburn and continuing to the west of it (for some distance virtually following a route later to be taken by the railway), then crossing the Eddleston Water at the village. From there the old road and today's followed the same line into Peebles.

An Act of 1771 allowed for improvements to roads radiating from Peebles, but it does not appear that any route changes were made at this time on the way to Edinburgh. It was not until about 1812 that the present road between Leadburn and Eddleston was made.

The Peebles road was often taken as an alternative route to Moffat, the obvious temptation being the number of inns there compared with the bare way through Broughton. The 1741 map shows a track through Stobo, crossing the Tweed by ford at Dawyck, but then stopping near Drumelzier. The 1771 Act probably made it possible for this to be made into a carriage road, extending it to cross the Tweed (again by ford) and reaching the Moffat road a mile south of Rachan Mill. Later the latter part of the route was changed when a bridge was built at Merlindale with a new road running to Rachan Mill.

On the way to Peebles, the inn at Leadburn has already been referred to in the previous chapter. At Eddleston, the Horseshoe Inn has been described as a coaching inn but as it only came into being in 1862 (having been formerly a smithy), it would have been too late by seven years to have served any stagecoaches, these having ceased running on the day the railway started in 1855. Their trade would have been derived from the users of private carriages.

In Peebles, the earliest Edinburgh coaches used the Harrow Inn in the High Street (later the Commercial and now the County Hotel), but some of the coaching business seems to have been shared with the Tontine a few doors away which opened for business in 1808. The Tontine had been built to meet the demand for additional accommodation in the town when the popular Cross Keys or Cleikum Inn in the Northgate (which dated from 1683) became inadequate.

There were tolls at Craigburn (replaced by Leadburn when the road was changed about 1812) and at Milkieston to the south of Eddleston.

Chapter 14

Cross Routes – Western Section

So far, all the routes dealt with have radiated in a broad arc southwards from Edinburgh into the Borders. To these must be added the many inter-connecting roads, including those which cross over the boundaries of the Borders to serve adjoining areas. Generally, only roads which were turnpiked have been included as they were the ones chosen at the time for upgrading to a standard capable of taking wheeled vehicles in most weather situations. There are exceptions however; some roads have been included where they had been originally turnpiked but are no longer there or are today of only minor importance, some others which were proposed for turnpiking although nothing came of it, and a small number of roads created in the post-turnpike era to cater for modern traffic demands.

For convenience, the entire Borders area has been divided into three arbitrary sections; the Western in this chapter covering the area west of Selkirk, the Central in chapter 15 for that part between Selkirk and Kelso and the Eastern in chapter 16 for the balance of the area to the east of Kelso. A number of roads start in one section and end in another and they appear in the one relevant to the first-named town.

The Western Section relates to the whole of Peeblesshire and most of Selkirkshire. Of the Border counties, these two seem to have been the poorest in medieval roads and other than the one over Minch Moor (see Glasgow to Selkirk below) only the smallest fragments have been discovered. This is probably because few of them were more than fair-weather tracks through and over the hills and were never improved nor had any constructional work associated with them.

Considering the small population thought to have lived in this area in the 16th, 17th and 18th centuries, it is somewhat surprising then to find a considerable number of unimproved roads from those times crossing over the many hills in the area. These are typical moorland roads, hollowed out or terraced depending on local conditions, often with two or more tracks over very difficult sections, having been created simply by the feet of men and animals. It is unlikely that wheeled vehicles, however primitive, could have been used on them. They were the Thief Roads of the reivers and later the drovers used them to take the small black Highland cattle on their way into England and on to London.

Even at the start of the 19th century, there were only three road bridges in Peeblesshire. The most important of these was the one at Peebles, the oldest of all the Tweed bridges above Berwick, originally constructed in the 15th century but rebuilt four times since then.. The second is at Tweedsmuir and although it carries the incised date 1783, it seems to have replaced an even older bridge there. The Tweed is quite narrow at this point, cascading over impressive rocks. The third is over the Lyne Water at Romanno Bridge. It was built in 1774 but is no longer in use, having been replaced, like so many others, by a modern structure to take today's traffic.

In Selkirkshire in 1800, apart from the Yair Bridge over the Tweed, there were only two road bridges and both were over the Ettrick Water, one was at Selkirk and the other appropriately at Ettrick Bridge End. The Selkirk one, built in 1777 and known locally as the Stane Brig, was destroyed by a disastrous flood in October 1977, requiring complete replacement. There had been a 17th century bridge over the Yarrow Water at Deuchar near Yarrow, but was destroyed in a flood in 1734 and is now no more than a picturesque ruin.

The Road to Biggar (A 702) – Map 12, C

Technically, this is the road from Edinburgh to Biggar, but as it penetrates the Borders for a mere six miles on its journey southwards, it has been included as a cross-route. The original road did not even serve any Border settlements on its way through, but later it was moved so that it did. Today this busy road gives a direct connection between Edinburgh and the M74 motorway through Clydesdale and Annandale into Carlisle and southwards.

As already dealt with in Chapter 2, the first road was an important Roman one connecting Carlisle, Annandale and the Forth valley. In medieval times it continued to be used and with much wear and repair, all signs of the Roman work gradually disappeared. The Turnpike Act of 1753 referred to improvements for the short Borders section of this road (as well as others serving Moffat) and about 1756 work was started causing further damage to what had remained of the Roman road. From the north, it entered the county at what is now Carlops (this village was a planned one and did not exist before 1784) and left it again near Dolphinton.

About 1831 plans were made for an entirely new road to run parallel to the old one but slightly further to the south-east to pass and serve West Linton and this was completed a few years later.

The one coaching inn on the Peeblesshire section of this road was the Bridge House Inn at West Linton and this might have been the same premises as Alexander's to which reference was made in the Edinburgh Post Office Directory.

There were two tolls on this road, these being at Carlops in the north and at Ingraston just before the road passed into Lanarkshire.

Glasgow to Selkirk (A721, A72 and A707) – Map 13

There are a number of permutations for the route from Glasgow through the Borders and this appears to have been the position from the earliest times. The first road from Clydesdale into the Borders would have been the Roman one to Trimontium but, as mentioned elsewhere, little of the actual way has survived and it is only west of Peebles that remains may still be seen. The conjectured way lay quite close to the present-day road to Carluke. It probably fell into disuse after the end of the Roman occupation and, even in medieval times, it may have been used only by people such as the monks of Kelso Abbey on the way to their property at places like Lesmahagow in Lanarkshire.

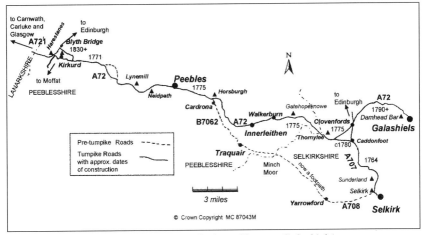

Map 13 – The Roads from Glasgow to Selkirk (and later to Galashiels).

The 1741 Edgar map of Peeblesshire shows a road *'from Glasgow to Peebles, Selkirk, Kelso and Jedburgh'* which for much of its way in the west of the county follows the route of today's A721 and A72 from Carluke and Carnwath. At Kirkurd, however, the road then went across by Castlecraig instead of the present way which turns north-east almost to Blyth Bridge before going south-east again to follow the valley of the Tarth Water. When the Lyne Water was reached, it was crossed by a ford and the road then kept to its east bank before joining the Tweed a short distance from Peebles.

At that time, the present road on the north bank of the Tweed never reached Innerleithen, for at Horsburgh it crossed the Tweed on a ford to pass Cardrona on the minor road south of the river. To go further east from Peebles then, either the traveller had to traverse this ford or, perhaps more likely, cross the river by the bridge at Peebles and follow the road to Cardrona and Traquair.

From Traquair the road left the valley of the Tweed to make the steep ascent of Minch Moor on its way to Selkirk. Later in the 18th century a stretch of this road became a busy part of the main drove road from Falkirk to England through the Borders. There were even plans to have it turnpiked as a major way eastwards from Traquair but this came to nothing although improvements were made to it in 1783 in anticipation. Today the well-marked track forms part of the long-distance footpath known as the Southern Uplands Way.

This route is one of the earliest to be recorded, for in 1305 the manor of Westerhope Kailzie was '*bound to give a man for eight days during Roxburgh Fair to keep the road through Minche Moor from robbers*'. – indicating the use of the way by travellers from the west to places as far east as Kelso. There was more than one track from Minch Moor to Selkirk, but the main one followed the Gruntly Burn to Yarrowford then by the road alongside the Yarrow Water. Writing in 1832, James Hogg refers to the ancient Thief or King's Road being kept open in his time for traffic over the Moor.

The Turnpike Act of 1771 covering the roads around Peebles included that section of the cross-route from the Lanarkshire border to the town itself. Much of the original way was retained as far as the Lyne Water, but instead of crossing it as before, the road now went down the west bank and crossed over on a new bridge close to the Roman fort at Lyne. Here it rejoined the former way and continued into Peebles.

Later, in the 1830s, a deviation was created to avoid the settlement of Kirkurd and the nearby Castlecraig Estate by having the road moved further to the north nearer Blyth Bridge.

East of Peebles, an earlier Act of 1768 created the authority for a new road on the north side of the Tweed and this was completed about 1775, giving a link with the emerging textile centres of Innerleithen and Walkerburn and continuing to the Selkirkshire boundary near Thornylee. In that county, a Trust had also been set about the same time to deal with this cross-road on its eastward way to Clovenfords, where it met the 1764 coach road from Edinburgh to Selkirk via Yair Bridge. Later, a new road was made by the Tweed west of Caddonfoot, so avoiding the journey to Clovenfords. The late-eighteenth century traveller would then have continued on to Selkirk to meet the other ways over Minch Moor already described.

The A72 winds its way along the Tweed Valley westwards towards Walkerburn.

In the 1790s, as Galashiels grew in importance, what had been a poor road from Clovenfords was improved to provide a way into the town from the west, so completing the last link in what was to become the A72. From then onwards, most traffic from Glasgow to the central and eastern Borders would now have gone by Galashiels rather than Selkirk.

The only coaching inns on this route were The Tontine and the Harrow at Peebles and, much later in the 1830s, Riddell's in Innerleithen which subsequently changed its name to the Traquair Arms Hotel. These would have been used in the main by private carriages on this route, for the first stagecoach to go this way (the Glasgow to Kelso service) did not start to operate until 1835.

There appears to be no evidence of a toll where this road enters Peeblesshire from the west, the first one being at Kirkurd at the junction with the (then) Edinburgh to Moffat Road. With the opening of the deviation there, a toll was moved to Harestanes at the new junction with the road from Edinburgh to Moffat. Between there and Peebles there were two tolls, one at Lynemill and the other at Neidpath close to the castle of the same name. East of Peebles the toll at Horsburgh had been moved around at least three times in its history, all within half a mile of one another.

Early in the 19th century, there had been a number of boundary changes between the counties of Peebles and Selkirk, necessitating the movement of a toll. Originally this had been at Holylee, but it was moved to Gatehopeknowe, a mile to the east of Walkerburn. Over the county boundary into Selkirkshire, the next toll was at Thornylee. The final toll before Selkirk was at Sunderland which was shared with the Carlisle road from Edinburgh.

The isolated toll house at Thornylee on the A72 between Innerleithen and Galashiels, close to the border between Selkirkshire and Peeblesshire.

At first there was no toll on the road from Clovenfords into Galashiels, but much later a toll known as Damhead Bar was built at the corner of what are now King and Duke Streets in Galashiels, less than half a mile of the town centre and close to the then boundary between the counties of Selkirk and Roxburgh.

Peebles to Hawick (B7062, B709, B711) – *Map 14, A*

This way was probably never conceived as a direct route between these two places, but grew haphazardly in the 18th century and became the quickest way to get from Peebles to upper Teviotdale. It was extensively used by drovers as one of the ways from the Pentland Hills to Hawick, but this town lost favour with them after 1777 and the route then took a more southerly way to Teviothead, joining what is now the main Carlisle road at Commonside, seven miles further upstream from Hawick.

The original road led from Peebles and followed the south bank of the Tweed as far as Traquair. Here it met a short spur from Innerleithen which crossed the river by a bridge which probably dates from about 1775 when the new road was built east of Peebles on the north side of the river. This bridge was replaced by the present structure in 1886.

From Traquair the original road took off for the hills near Traquair Church, about a mile south of the village, on its way to Dryhope close by St. Mary's Loch. This road is described by Roy in his 1750 map as *'the Muir road from the head of Yarrow and Ettrick to Lothian Edge and Dalkeith'*. By the late 18th century, the road took a more direct way, following the Paddock Burn (at one time known as Newhall Burn) until the watershed and the Selkirkshire boundary, then down the Mountbenger Burn to cross the Selkirk to Moffat road where the Gordon Arms Hotel is now. Known locally by the name Paddy Slacks, this stretch of road has associations with historical and literary figures. One popular derivation of the name is from Pas des Lacs, said to have been used by the French retinue of Mary Queen of Scots when they rode with her to the forest. Certainly there are two 'lakes' near the end of the original road over the hills, but not on the one which today carries the name. It is much more likely that it is taken from the local feature Paddock Slack, Paddock being the name of the burn and Slack meaning a hollow between hills or a boggy area. What is much more certain is that this was the road taken by Hogg and his visitor Wordsworth when they walked together in 1814.

From the Gordon Arms the road crossed over the hills to Tushielaw in the Ettrick valley where it joined the Selkirk to Ettrick road for a short distance before starting on the final part of its journey to Hawick on a road built about 1826. It passes the small settlement of Roberton on its way to join the Carlisle road only a mile south of Hawick. Most of the present road follows the original way, except for a stretch a few miles to the south-east of Tushielaw. Originally the road had gone over the high ground to the north of Craig Hill, but a new way followed the Rankle Burn to Buccleuch, meeting the old one again further east.

The first inn on the road was the Gordon Arms (now Gordon Arms Hotel) at Mountbenger, where the road crossed the one from Selkirk to Moffat. It dates from about 1820 and although there appears to have been no provision for the hiring and stabling of horses, it was a popular stopping place on both roads. The next was in the Ettrick valley at Tushielaw where the road joined the one from Selkirk for a short distance before leaving it for Hawick. The Tushielaw Inn, which still operates today, is described as a coaching inn, but there was no stagecoach service on either road in the heyday of this form of traffic and it was probably only private carriages which called here. It has been suggested that the Yarrow coach which started in 1887 may have used a circular route to include part of the Ettrick valley and if this is the case, it could well have stopped at Tushielaw.

Greenbank Toll, on the B711 between Buccleuch and Roberton, showing the unusual shape of the walls to enable the tollkeeper to see the roadway in both directions.

The first toll was at Kailzie a few miles to the east of Peebles. A toll was erected at the north end of the old Tweed Bridge at Innerleithen and this was retained when the new bridge was built in 1886. There were also tolls at Newhall, close by the boundary between of Peeblesshire with Selkirkshire and at Mountbenger and Tushielaw, all three probably there primarily to deal with drovers and their cattle rather than wheeled transport. On the final stretch to Hawick, there was an unusual toll-house at Greenbank Farm to the west of Roberton, built in 1826 at the same time as the road. An extension to a building at Greenbank Farm, it had five sides with windows placed in positions to give the best views of oncoming traffic in either direction. It can still be seen today, although by 1865 it had ceased to be used as a toll.

Map 14 – Peebles to Hawick, Moffat to Selkirk and Langholm to Selkirk.

Moffat through the Yarrow Valley to Selkirk (A708) – Map 14, B

It is doubtful whether this attractive route ever rivalled the other Moffat road through Peeblesshire which carried the bulk of traffic to the spa from Edinburgh and it was possibly nothing more than a connection to the central and eastern Borders. In Dumfriesshire it followed the valley of the Moffat Water as far as the watershed at the Selkirkshire boundary, then that of the Yarrow Water for the entire length until it joins the Ettrick to the west of Selkirk. Although the general way has not changed all that amount in the course of time, old maps do show that the route did alter.

Today the way lies on the north (or left) bank of the Yarrow, but Roy's Military Map of 1750 shows the road going along the south-east side of St. Mary's Loch and crossing the water by a ford near Dryhope. Ainslie's map of 1773 shows a road on the north-west shore of the loch in addition to the one on the other side, but by the time Thomson's map appeared in 1834, the south-east shore road had gone.

Allowing for inaccuracies which crept into old maps, it does appear that in earlier times parts of this road may have been further from the water than is the case today. Despite this, the road was often flooded. In the 1790s the local minister referred to the bad state of the roads in the parish of Yarrow and '*that they require great amendments.....frequently the traveller, by the swelling of the rivers, is either obstructed altogether upon his route or obliged to go many miles about, in order to pursue his journey*'.

The only other route alteration of note was carried out in the late 19th century when the road through Broadmeadows at Yarrowford was diverted over two bridges to produce a short way on the south bank.

No scheduled coaches used this route until 1887 and in the early days anyone brave enough to have taken a private carriage on it would have found the lack of facilities somewhat daunting. Two inns did appear in the early 1800s but whether they were ever adequately equipped to deal with anything more than refreshing the occupants of carriages is not at all clear. The famous Tibby Shiel's Inn at the head of St. Mary's Loch is slightly off the Moffat road but would have been adjacent to the former road on the south-east side of the loch. It became an inn about 1820, probably in the same decade as the road was moved to the other side of the water.

Nearer Selkirk, there is the Gordon Arms Hotel at Mountbenger which has already been dealt with under the previous heading.

As this road was never the subject of a turnpike act, there were no tolls along it.

Langholm through the Tima and Ettrick Valleys to Selkirk (B709 and B7009) – Map 14, C

Like the Yarrow road, this one also closely followed the course of a Tweed tributary, in this case the Ettrick in its picturesque valley. In Roy's map it is shown as the road to Moffat, although quite likely it was no more than a mere track in the 1750s. Whereas today's road branches south at Ettrick to follow the Tima Water into Eskdale, at that time this section did not exist, the road instead continuing up the Ettrick valley and crossing into Dumfriesshire to join the Selkirk to Moffat road about six miles north of the latter town. By 1773 Ainslie's map shows a track alongside the Tima Water and this is enthusiastically marked 'Road to Carlisle down Eskdale'.

James Hogg, who was born in Ettrick in 1770, summed up the state of the roads when he wrote '*there was not a single carriage-road through the county save the London Mail road that intersects a part of it by Selkirk. There were a few narrow paths, formed here and there leading to Gentlemen's Houses, but no communication through the county by any other'*. As the London mailcoach service through Selkirk did not start to operate until 1806, he was obviously speaking about a time after that date. Slightly earlier in the 1790s, the OSA mentioned that the roads are almost impassable – *'The only road that looks like a turnpike is to Selkirk, but even it in so many places is so deep, as greatly to obstruct travelling. The distance is about 16 miles and it requires four hours to ride it..... snow also at times a great inconvenience..... another great disadvantage is the want of bridges.'*

It was Lord Napier (William 9th Baron) who did much to improve Selkirkshire roads when he settled in the county about 1820 and it was shortly after that when the Tima valley section of this road was made capable of taking carriage traffic. Even at that time, the Moffat link still appeared on the map although it had never been improved. Today it remains as a footpath which forms part of the Southern Uplands Way. From Ettrick the road to Selkirk follows the north bank of the Ettrick Water past Tushielaw where it crosses the road from Traquair to Hawick. At Ettrickbridge, the river is crossed and the way continued on the south bank.

At Inner Huntly, the modern road continues to follow the Ettrick Water but originally it went over the hill by the Roman fort to return to the river at Howden, only a short distance from Selkirk. By 1824 both routes were shown in Thomson's map and it was probably shortly after that when the hill road went out of use as part of the route. Today sections of the way still exist as public roads servicing farms. On the old road, near Hartwoodmyres, there is a branch called Woll Rig which marks part of what is considered to have been an ancient way from Selkirk to Hawick through Ashkirk.

The only inn and toll-house on this road were in the same premises at Tushielaw. The inn has already been referred to and the toll was there primarily to cater for traffic (especially driven cattle) on the north-south road from Peebles to Hawick. Like the Yarrow road, this one was never turnpiked.

The Roads to Innerleithen from the North (B7007 and B709) – *Map 15*

There are two ways to Innerleithen over the Moorfoot Hills from the north; one off the A7 at Middleton Hall in Midlothian (the B7007) and the other (the B709) again off the A7, but near Heriot House, at one time also in Midlothian but now forming part of the Borders. These two roads meet near Garvald Lodge and the way continues southwards to Innerleithen as the B709. There is archaeological evidence of a track following the same way which may have been used from early times, but it does not appear in the Edgar's 1741 map and even in 1775 Armstrong

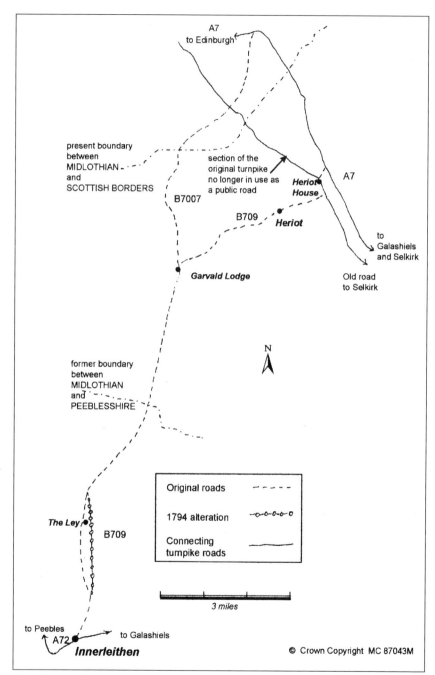

Map 15 – Innerleithen Roads.

showed the way merely as a bridle road. In 1794, however, this was replaced by a new road which was built by subscription for the carriage of lime and coal to the district.

Little appears to be known about subsequent events in the 19th century and as far as can be ascertained, it was never the subject of a turnpike act. The present road probably follows the route of the 1775 one for most of the way, but as it approaches the town down the Leithen Water, it now lies on the east bank whereas the old road was on the west side through The Ley.

Stagecoaches never used this road and it is doubtful whether many private carriages went this way as its maintenance would never have been up to turnpike standards. It was the introduction of private cars that helped to turn it into a modern road and today it is the way used by the people who commute daily to Edinburgh from their homes in the Innerleithen district.

The Road to Biggar through Skirling (A72) and Biggar to Broughton (B7016) – Map 12, E

These two roads run quite close together and provide links between Biggar and the A701 Edinburgh to Moffat highway. Neither is very old, both being products of the Turnpike Act of 1771. This area close to the Lanarkshire border was well used by drovers in connection with local markets at Biggar and Skirling and it is likely that the indifferent tracks shown in Ainslie's map of 1773 were principally used for this purpose. It was well into the 19th century before any significant improvements were made to enable carriages to be used. The latter road was described by the parish minister in the NSA of 1830 as having been the worst piece of road in that part of the county, although *'now in a fair way of being soon in good order'*.

Drove Road over the Pentland Hills at Cauldstane Slap – Map 12

Although drove roads became important in the middle of the 18th century when Highland cattle began to be sent to markets in England, it is apparent that this one is older than that, for in Roy's Military Map of 1750 it is shown as the 'road to Queensferry'. In 1830 attempts were made to make this part of a new route to Falkirk, Stirling and Queensferry from the Borders and to this end, part of the way from West Linton to Baddinsgill was metalled. Nothing came of this novel project and this is the only part of the way open to traffic – well worth a visit to admire the Pentlands scenery.

Chapter 15

Cross Routes – Central Section

The Central Section, representing the arbitrary part between Selkirk and Kelso, contains about two-thirds of the population of the Borders, most of them in the five towns of Hawick, Galashiels, Selkirk, Kelso and Jedburgh and the surrounding fertile lands of the Tweed basin. Unsurprisingly, most of the industries too are found here. With the exception of Galashiels (a small village before the arrival of the textile industry) all are towns with a long history, but until the middle of the 18th century the demands for roads to serve them were never very great. They are closely connected with the Tweed either directly or by a tributary and it was the river system which caused many of the early problems in creating new roads. Bridges were a rarity, with early ones near Melrose and Kelso being destroyed for strategic reasons and not replaced until the 1750s.

Away from the population belt in the Tweed valley, the north is dominated by the Lammermuir Hills and the south by the wild country leading into Liddesdale, the last part of the Borders to get roads capable of taking any form of wheeled traffic.

Selkirk to St. Boswells and Kelso (A699) – *Map 16, A*

In historical terms, the present road as far as St. Boswells is not old, unlike the section on to Kelso which goes back to medieval times. In the 18th century, the way took an easterly path from the top end of Selkirk to Midlem, Clarilaw and Longnewton, then crossed the Edinburgh to Jedburgh road to reach Maxton.

It appears that the road was kept in poor repair and this, coupled with very rough ground for much of the way, meant that travellers from Selkirk to Kelso were usually obliged to go by Melrose. Writing in 1815, William Scott of Raeburn (convenor of the newly-formed Selkirk and St. Boswells Turnpike Trust) noted that the existing length of road was no more than a bridle path and that even in the summer months carriages had to struggle.

Alexander Kinghorne, a road engineer from St. Boswells, had been asked to look at feasible options for an entirely new road and in his 1813 report he mentioned three possible routes, the recommended one being that eventually selected, so producing the one substantially in use today. The cost would amount to £1544. Of the total distance of eight and a quarter miles between Selkirk and St. Boswells, only two were in Selkirkshire, so although there was a toll at the western end of the road in that county, the trustees there had to remit a hefty two-thirds of the income from it to the Selkirk and St. Boswells Trust.

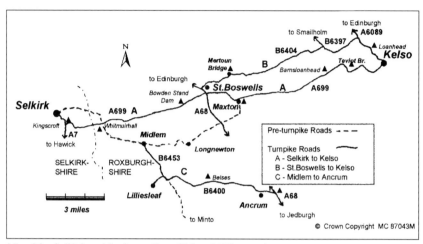

Map 16 – Selkirk and St. Boswells to Kelso; Midlem to Ancrum.

The new road started off just as the old one had done, in an easterly direction from Selkirk, but then took a new way north of Midlem and, making directly for St. Boswells, met the Edinburgh to Jedburgh road just to the south of the village. From there a new section was created to nearby Maxton to meet with the older road. Later, a better way out of Selkirk was made with a new road being built off the one to Hawick, so completing the road which is with us today.

The road east of Maxton towards Kelso is a much older route, dating from the earliest times; until the Mertoun Bridge was completed in 1841, this was the only practical way from the central Borders to that town. In Stobie's 1770 map of Roxburghshire the route shown for most of the way follows exactly today's A699 (allowing for minor modern realignments) and it is only at the Kelso end that things have changed. Originally the entry into Kelso was effected by a ford on the Tweed between Friar's Haugh and the north end of the town, that part then known as Wester Kelso.

There may have been plans to build a bridge at this site to replace the ford, but if so nothing came of it. Instead, proposals were made to have the bridge over the Teviot and a design for this was submitted in 1784, the cost at that time being £1000. This new bridge was intended to provide an entry to the town by carrying the road to join the one from Hawick close by the Kelso bridge which had been erected earlier in 1754. The necessary act of parliament was obtained in 1793 to improve the entire way from St. Boswells and to build the bridge, work on which was completed in 1795. Two years later, Kelso bridge was swept away in a devastating flood, effectively cutting off both routes from the town. If traffic was unable to use the fords or the reintroduced ferries, then it was a long and tedious detour until the new bridge was built in 1803.

The Teviot Bridge of 1795 on the Selkirk road near Kelso, showing the adjacent toll house.

There were three tolls on the section between Selkirk and St. Boswells; the first at Kingscroft where the road left the one to Hawick, then at Whitmuirhall close to the boundary between the counties of Selkirk and Roxburgh and at the cross-roads near Bowden which was known as Bowden Stand Dam.

East of St. Boswells, there were tolls at Maxton village and at Barnsloanhead where the road from Roxburgh village joined, but the latter one was closed when the Teviot Bridge and the adjacent toll there were completed in 1795.

St. Boswells to Kelso via Mertoun (B6404) – Map 16, B

There appears to have been a demand for a road to Kelso from the Central Borders to go along the north side of the Tweed. Fragments of a way had existed before, but the main obstacle was the Tweed itself. The matter was resolved in 1841 with the completion of a bridge at Mertoun with a new road connecting it to Lessudden, as St. Boswells was then known. On the Kelso side of the bridge, use was made of existing farmtracks which were then improved to the standards of the time, and extended eastwards to meet the Smailholm to Kelso road near Charterhouse. The original bridge at Mertoun was timber-built with stone piers and it was only later that the present attractive structure with its five masonry arches replaced it. At the same time, a toll was incorporated, the only one on this stretch of road.

Few mileage markers survive on Border roads; this metal one is on the road between St. Boswells and Kelso.

Apart from the inevitable widening and surface improvements, the only alteration to the road was in the early 1930s when a new short way was created near Clintmains, cutting across three right-angle bends to improve the route.

Midlem to Ancrum Toll (B6453, B6400) – Map 16, C

This little-known and somewhat modest turnpike appears to have been all that was ever built of an abortive new road to connect Melrose to Hawick through Bowden, Midlem, Minto and Wilton. This was the subject of an act of parliament in 1819 and the following year advertisements appeared for contractors to tender for ditching and paling of the proposed highway, but this was the last to be heard of the project.

In 1770 few of the roads which made up the route between Midlem and Ancrum Toll had even existed, so much of the work done was completely new. There had been an existing track from Midlem southwards in the direction of Minto, but near Lilliesleaf a new way went through the settlement of Belses to Ancrum to meet the Edinburgh to Jedburgh road at Ancrum Toll. A short spur to Lilliesleaf completed the simple turnpike system.

Apart from Ancrum Toll, the only other one was at Belses.

Galashiels to Newtown (B6374, A6091) – Map 17

Until late in the 18th century, the village of Galashiels was an insignificant one on the way to nowhere, avoided by cross-country traffic in every direction. The growing textile industry in the Borders depended on a good supply of water to power the machinery in the mills which were to replace the looms in the homes of the workers – and it was the swift flow of the Gala Water which turned Galashiels into what is now the second largest town in the Borders.

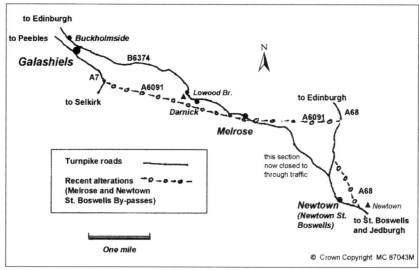

Map 17 – Galashiels to Newtown.

In 1755 the population of the town was 827, much smaller than places such as Lauder and Earlston, and even by 1801 this had only grown to 844. By 1881 however it had risen to 9472, but this is not a true picture, for at that time the boundary between Selkirkshire and Roxburghshire lay along the Gala Water which goes through the heart of the modern town, so anyone living north of it would have been included in the population for the parish of Melrose. It was only later that this part including the textile village of Buckholmside was brought within the ambit of Selkirkshire to give a clearer and more accurate picture of the growth of the town.

In chapter 11 dealing with the road from Edinburgh to Selkirk and Carlisle, reference was made to the new one built on the east bank of the Gala Water in 1818. At Bowland, where the road left the valley to go southwards to Clovenfords, an extension to Galashiels had been built, descending the valley and crossing the Gala by what was described as a very dangerous bridge. Just to the north of this bridge, an old road to Melrose had gone eastwards and this was used for part of the way of the new turnpike planned in the Act of 1793 to connect Galashiels with Newtown (now Newtown St. Boswells) where it would meet with the highway connecting Edinburgh with Jedburgh.

Melrose Bridge, sometimes known as Lowood or Bottle Bridge, built in 1762 as part of the turnpike road between Galashiels and Newtown. Still in use today but now of diminished importance since the completion of the Melrose bypass.

The road followed the north bank of the Tweed for about a mile before crossing it at Lowood on a handsome double-arched bridge built by Laidlaw and Purves of Kelso in 1762 to replace the one half a mile downstream which had been destroyed by floods a few years before. To save money, stone from the remains of the old bridge was used in the construction of the new one. The chosen site had good bedrock for the foundations and it was found that using the new site would have been cheaper than rebuilding on the old one. The cost was met by contributions from all the landowners of Roxburghshire in proportion to their rental income.

The popular name of this elegant structure is Bottle Bridge, apparently so called because a bottle of contemporary coins had been built into it by the masons. The bridge was substantially altered in 1897, being closed for four months for the replacement of the upper parts. It was a few years too early for the authorities to have anticipated the need for a broader carriageway; the motor-car and bus had not yet arrived on the scene. It remains in use today, despite being far too narrow to cope with modern traffic and is one of the handful of Borders bridges controlled by traffic-signals to give alternate one-way working.

On the other side, the road joined up with the one from Selkirk at Darnick and went the short distance into Melrose. From there it passed round the lower slopes of the North Hill of the Eildons, more or less following the medieval way to Jedburgh and creating a notorious stretch as it passed the little valley formed by the Bogle Burn just before Eildon village. From there it descended to join the main road from Edinburgh to Jedburgh at the top end of Newtown.

In chapters 21 and 22, it will be shown how this route was the one chosen to take the Edinburgh coaches to Melrose and Jedburgh and later all the way to London over Carter Bar.

Until the 1980s, this way remained intact, creating many problems for modern traffic, but these were resolved when an entirely new road was constructed east of Galashiels, with a bridge over the Tweed to connect the Selkirk to Galashiels road with the one from Selkirk to Darnick on the other side of the river. The new bridge was built quite close to the old ford which in coaching days had been a dubious alternative to those who did not want to take the longer journey by Lowood Bridge. This then became the start of the Melrose bypass, making use of the route of the closed railway line. East of Melrose, the old road continued to be used until 1996 when the final work was completed to take the road eastwards to the Jedburgh road (A68) at a point about a mile north of Newtown St. Boswells. By then it had already been bypassed, so that there were no towns or villages to be gone through between Galashiels and St. Boswells. The Bogle Burn road was closed, as was the former connection between the village of Newstead and the A68 at Leaderfoot.

The road from Newtown St. Boswells to Melrose at the Bogle Burn, now closed to traffic since the completion of the Melrose bypass in 1996.

The coaching inns on this road were Jones' at Buckholmside (later known as the Ladhope Inn and still there) to serve the people of Galashiels and the George (now the George and Abbotsford) at Melrose. Both had been built early in the 19th century to handle the coach traffic on the Jedburgh route to and from Edinburgh.

There was already a toll-house at Lowood Bridge before the turnpike road was built (the pontage raised being used to maintain the structure) and this was retained by the trustees. There were no other tolls on the road itself, but close by at either end there were established ones at Whitelee (Whitlaw) and at Newtown which would have been unavoidable by most of the travellers going this way.

Hawick to Newcastleton (B6399, B6357) – Map 18, A

There are no old records of a roadway on this route prior to the 18th century, but the entire area of hills and moorland was probably criss-crossed with tracks used by generations of reivers and their pursuers. Today's road ascends the valley of the Slitrig Water (a tributary of the Teviot) as far as the watershed, then descends by the Hermitage Water to its junction with the Liddel to join the Jedburgh road just before Newcastleton. From there it is only a short distance to the Dumfriesshire border and on to Canonbie, Longtown and Carlisle. The austere 14th century Hermitage Castle close to this road serves as a grim reminder of the past.

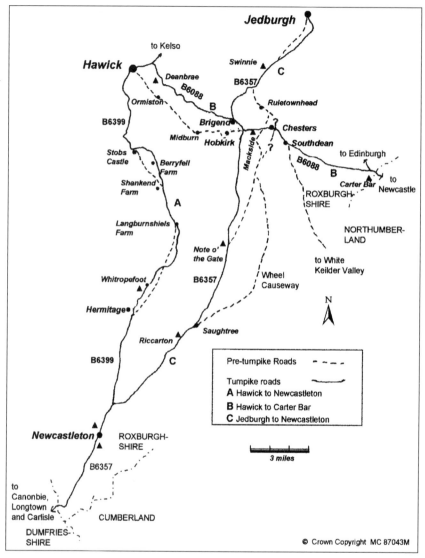

Map 18 – Hawick and Jedburgh to Newcastleton; Hawick to Carter Bar.

Newcastleton, the most southerly settlement in Roxburghshire, was laid out as a weaving village by the Duke of Buccleuch in 1793 to replace the original Castleton further upstream which has now disappeared.

The road first appeared in Stobie's map of 1770, very roughly following the modern B6399 except for two deviations. The first was between Stobs Castle and Shankend where both roads were obliged to leave the river because of the narrow gorge. The old road went eastwards but to the west side of Berryfell Farm, whereas the modern way takes an even more easterly route to the other side of the farm. The second was a little further south at Langburnshiels, taking a direct route to Hermitage, while today's road takes a slightly longer one, presumably to find easier gradients for wheeled traffic.

The OSA of 1793 gives a clear picture of what conditions were like at that time:

> 'Castletown:It must appear very strange to any person acquainted with the improvements, which other parts of Scotland have received by means of roads, when it is mentioned that in this very extensive country, not a yard of road has ever been attempted to be formed till with the last few years. For about 16 miles along the Liddal, the road lay rather in the river than upon its banks, the only path being in what is called the Watergate, and the unhappy traveller must cross it at least 24 times in that extent. The same thing still takes place, with respect to the Hermitage as far as it runs. To get to Hawick and Langholm markets, every article must be carried on horseback; and through these deep and broken bogs and mosses we must crawl, to the great fatigue of ourselves, but the much greater injury to our horses. Until 1792 there were no bridges in the parish, either the Liddal or the Hermitage.'

That matters had improved considerably by 1800 is evidenced by the fact that Walter Scott's wife Charlotte, according to a contemporary letter-writer, 'rode triumphantly in her strong, light, low phaeton – astonishing the good natives, for it was the first wheeled carriage that ever penetrated into Liddesdale'. Another account of the incident mentioned that Scott himself was there as well on this occasion and perhaps his wife tended to get most of the publicity as she was showing off the new carriage recently bought for her in London and shipped to Leith.

There was one coaching inn, the Liddesdale at Newcastleton, which may have been the destination of Lady Scott's ride. There was a toll-gate at Whitropefoot north of Hermitage and another at the approaches to Newcastleton , known as at Castleton Townhead. At the south of the town was another toll (Castleton Townfoot) to attend to the traffic going towards the Dumfriesshire border.

Hawick to Carter Bar (A6088) – Map 18, B

The old road to the south-east of Hawick had started off from the centre of the town, passing Ormiston and Midburn and crossing the Jedburgh to Newcastleton road near to where a toll-house was later built at Mackside. At Chesters, it then turned to the south-east and at Southdean it followed the Black Burn to enter England at Knox Knowe on its way into the valley of the White Keilder.

Realising the advantage of using the good road over the Cheviots at Carter Bar, the trustees planned an entirely new route from Hawick which made little use of the old one. Started in 1836, it left the Kelso road about one and a half miles to the north-east of the town passing Deanbrae, roughly parallel to the old road, but taking advantage of valleys to ease gradients. Shortly before crossing the Rule Water, it joined another new road (Jedburgh to Newcastleton) and it was here in the parish of Hobkirk that a settlement grew up, known at first as Bridgend or Brigend but later as Bonchester Bridge.

The old route was followed through Chesters and Southdean before an entirely new way was taken over the moors to join the Jedburgh road within a short distance from the English boundary. The connection between Hawick and Redesdale was now complete and most of the old road fell into disuse.

There was an inn called Bridgend near Hobkirk which was to become today's Horse and Hounds at Bonchester Bridge. It has been described as a coaching inn, but the trade must have been very erratic with perhaps only the occasional private carriage making the effort on such a poor road.

There were two tolls, one at Deanbrae about a mile up the hill from the Kelso road, the other at Mackside between Hobkirk and Chesters.

Jedburgh to Newcastleton (B6357) – Map 18, C

The first road between Jedburgh and Liddesdale would have been the medieval Wheel Causeway described in chapter 3. Later another road appeared which ran further west of Chesters and made its way to Note o' the Gate. The derivation of this name, no more than a dot on the map, is not known and it might have been forgotten today had it not been for the fact that this was a resting-place for Prince Charlie and his army on their advance into England in 1745. Today it lies deep in the man-made Wauchope Forest. From there the way went to Saughtree and the valley of the Liddle. This was the road mentioned by Thomas Gardner in 1719 when he published his road map from Carlisle to Berwick by way of Jedburgh and Kelso, suggesting perhaps that at that time this was a better way than the alternative through Langholm and Hawick.

When the need became evident for a carriage road, work started in the 1790s on a radically-changed route. The old way out of Jedburgh had left the town on what is now the Hawick road, but soon branched off to the south to Swinnie then to Ruletownhead. Now it came off the Carter Bar road south of the town on a new way to Swinnie then south-westwards to Brigend (now Bonchester Bridge) where it met the Hawick to Carter Bar turnpike. Just to the east of there, it branched off again to follow the valley of the Hyndlee Burn, meeting the former way at Note o' the Gate. Descending by the valley of the Dawston Burn to the Liddel at Saughtree, it then continued by the Liddel Water until the Hawick road was reached just to the north of Newcastleton.

Apart from the inn at Brigend, there were no others on the road until Newcastleton, perhaps the best indicator that few carriages used it. Along the way, toll houses were built at Swinnie, Note o' the Gate and Riccarton.

Hawick to Kelso (A698) – Map 19

This road formed the central part of the way from Carlisle to Berwick, one which came into prominence in the middle of the 18th century. Generally, it followed the right bank of the Teviot but at a safe distance or height from a river which has always been notorious for flooding. Shortly after passing through Denholm, the road divided at Spittal, the main road continuing to follow the river and the other for Jedburgh turning eastwards to cross over by Dunion Hill and into that town.

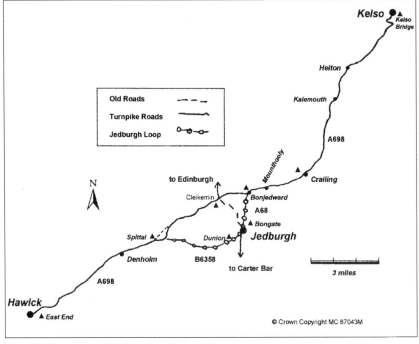

Map 19 – Hawick and Jedburgh to Kelso.

At Cleikemin, the road from Edinburgh to Jedburgh was crossed and shortly afterwards the one from Jedburgh to Kelso was joined at Bonjedward . The Jed Water and the vestige of Dere Street were crossed at Mounthooly and, passing through the village of Crailing at the edge of the Teviot floodplain, the way continued on to Heiton and Kelso. It is thought that originally the entry into Kelso was not as now by Maxwellheugh but by a lower road through what was to become Springwood Estate. The move to the present way might have been about the time of the laying out of Springwood Park in the 1750s, which coincides with the construction of the first Kelso Bridge in 1754. From the bridge the road entered Kelso by Belmont Place and Abbey Close (now Abbey Court) and on to the Market Square.

In 1768 the required turnpike act was obtained to improve the road. Few directional changes were made but the usual rebuilding in places was probably necessary to cater for the amount of wheeled traffic expected. Spittal was bypassed, the revised road now crossing the Rule Water slightly higher up the hill. Perhaps there had been a flooding problem here before.

The toll house at Spittal on the A698 between Hawick and Kelso, near the junction with the road to Jedburgh. The building is now used as a farm store and the filled-in window openings have been skilfully painted to give the impression of their former use.

Following the destruction of Kelso Bridge in the disastrous flood of 1797, a replacement was completed in 1803 to the design of John Rennie, the son of an East Lothian farmer, who went on to design and build bridges throughout Britain. These included the famous Waterloo Bridge in London, of which his Kelso one was the prototype. The new five-arched bridge and associated toll-house were completed a few yards downstream from the old one and this meant a new way into the town close by the ruins of the Abbey, appropriately called Bridge Street.

In the 1850s, as already explained in chapter 9, the section of road between Cleikemin and Bonjedward came to be used by both routes when the old road over the hill to Jedburgh was closed. It was not until 1940 that the Ancrum Bridge was replaced, resulting in today's road pattern.

During the last thirty years, the rapid growth in traffic has led to many improvements on this road, notably on the Hawick to the A68 section where awkward corners (but not all) have been straightened out with much widening and regrading. East of the A68, the most obvious changes occurred at Crailing which was bypassed and at Mounthooly and Kalemouth where old bridges were replaced and approaches improved.

Kelso Bridge, suffering badly from overuse by heavy vehicles with no alternative way to go, is at the time of writing being replaced by a new structure further downstream and when this has been completed, there will be an effective bypass to keep through traffic out of the town. Fortunately the Rennie Bridge will remain in use for local light traffic.

Unless a deviation was made to the Spread Eagle at Jedburgh (see below), there were no coaching inn facilities on the road between Hawick and Kelso. The first tollhouse was at Hawick East End, followed by others at Spittal (at the junction with the road to Jedburgh), Cleikemin (sometimes known as Cleekum) where the Edinburgh to Jedburgh road crossed over, Crailing and finally at the Tweed Bridge in Kelso. In the 1850s a further toll was erected at Bonjedward to replace the one at Cleikemin when the route of the Edinburgh to Jedburgh road was moved.

Hawick to Kelso via Jedburgh (B6358) – Map 19

This deviation was the way chosen for the stagecoach which ran between Hawick and Kelso, changing horses at the Spread Eagle. It left the direct route at Spittal and rose almost 600 feet to cross by Dunion Hill and down into Jedburgh past the castle and into the Lawnmarket.

Originally, the way out of Jedburgh followed the old Edinburgh road past Sharplaw, then turned to descend to Bonjedward, where it joined the direct road from Hawick to Kelso. When the present A68 route was laid out in the 1850s, this was then followed, again as far as Bonjedward, before turning off for Kelso.

There were tollhouses at Dunion less than a mile above Jedburgh and at Bongate on the way out of the town.

Chapter 16

Cross Routes – Eastern Section

This section covers eastern Roxburghshire and the greater part of Berwickshire. With the exception of that part in the area of the Lammermuirs in the north, this is the richest farmland in the whole Borders area. To a greater extent than elsewhere, the road pattern has been decided by the needs of farming rather than those of passers-by and this has resulted in an extensive network of minor roads, public and private. Apart from Dunglass on the Great North Road, there are no surviving ancient bridges and the first over the Tweed in the area was not until 1766 at Coldstream.

Earlston to Duns (A6105) – *Map 20, A*

Earlston to Greenlaw

Surprisingly, this section of the road did not exist until the late 1830s, making it one of the last to be created in today's network of Border roads. In the NSA for Earlston written in 1834, the minister deplores the absence of such a route, saying that '*the facilities of communication would be still further increased were a line of road made from Fans through the waste land eastward to the neighbouring parish of Gordon*'. The eventual road did go to Gordon (or West Gordon as it was then known) then on to Greenlaw, but did not pass by Fans, taking instead a more northerly way by Huntlywood to avoid the extensive boggy area which lay to the west of Gordon. The final section to Greenlaw avoided the worst of the bogs, reaching the town from the south and joining the Edinburgh to Coldstream road at the bridge over the Blackadder Water.

At that time, serious consideration was being given to the future of tolls and perhaps, reflecting this, none was ever built on this section.

Greenlaw to Duns

This is a much older road, appearing on Armstrong's 1771 map and taking a route almost the same as the present road. Rising above the town, it formed a boundary between the wastes of Greenlaw Moor and the Marchmont estate which had been laid out in the middle of the 18th century. From Polwarth, it continued past Gavinton and into Duns (Dunse in those days) from the south-west.

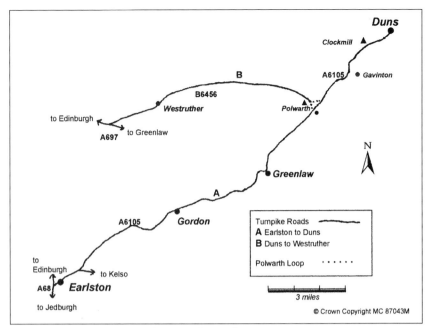

Map 20 – Earlston to Duns and Duns to Westruther.

All the roads around Duns (including this one) were turnpiked in 1793 but it appears that no route changes were made at that time. Only later about 1830 was a new road built for a short distance at Polwarth to cut off the loop to Polwarth Mill. Various improvements were also made to the approaches to Duns but these were minor in character.

The two tolls were at Polwarth Mill (until this was by-passed by the new road) and at Clockmill on the way into Duns.

Duns to Westruther (B6456) – *Map 20, B*

A road created by a Turnpike Act of 1803 to fulfil the joint purposes of supplying an alternative route to Duns from the west and giving a communication to the outside world for the isolated small village of Westruther. Going westwards from Duns, the new road went off from the Greenlaw road at Polwarth Mill and climbed into the moors and foothills of the Lammermuirs to Westruther. From there it passed close to the Spottiswoode estate to rejoin the Greenlaw road within a mile of the inn at Whiteburn. The only toll was at Polwarth Mill which served both the new road and the one from Greenlaw to Duns.

Kelso to Coldstream (A698) – *Map 21, A*

Today this road forms a vital part of cross-country communication and it is hard to believe that its importance in the 18th century was so slight that the decision to have it turnpiked was not made until 1793, almost thirty years after most of the major ways in and out of Kelso were completed. Roy's military map of 1750 shows hardly anything more than the merest track north of the Tweed in an easterly direction.

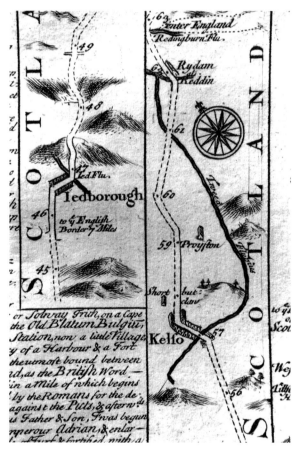

Part of one of the earliest road maps of the Borders, made by Thomas Gardner in 1719, showing in strip form two sections of the road between Carlisle and Berwick through Jedburgh and Kelso. At mileage-mark 62, the Tweed is crossed by a ford, all traces of which have now gone.

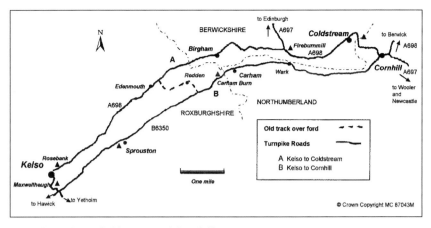

Map 21 – Kelso to Coldstream and Cornhill.

An early road-map of the Carlisle to Berwick road produced by Thomas Gardner in London in 1719 formed part of a traveller's guide for all important routes in England and Wales and included the one incursion into Scotland where the road from Carlisle to Berwick went through Jedburgh and Kelso. The map clearly shows a road leaving Kelso, but then crossing the Tweed by a ford at Edenmouth, passing Redden Farm and joining what is now the south bank road close to the border with England. Armstrong's fine 1771 map of Berwickshire indicates that there had been a ford there and gives a further pointer by the fact that the eastwards road peters out just as the Eden Water is reached. From there to near Lochton Farm (or Loughtoun as shown on the map) only a track is shown. At Lochton it becomes a road again through Birgham and on to Fireburnmill where it joined the Greenlaw to Coldstream turnpike on its way into the latter town.

The Act of 1793 created the means to improve the way, including the provision of a bridge over the Eden near Edenmouth. Essentially this is the same road used today, the only obvious improvement since then being the recent construction of a new bridge at Edenmouth to replace the narrow one which still stands adjacent to it.

The tolls were at Rosebank on the way out of Kelso and at Fireburnmill. The boundary between the counties of Roxburgh and Berwick lies about halfway along this road and it is rather unusual that a toll was never built there. Perhaps by the end of the 18th century, the authorities began to realise that too many tollhouses were beginning to become counter-productive as people found ways of avoiding them whenever possible. In this case one at either end of the road was considered sufficient.

Travellers crossing the Tweed by Coldstream Bridge then had the options of turning left after Cornhill to make for Berwick or right for Wooler, Morpeth, Newcastle and other points further south.

Kelso to Cornhill (B6350) – Map 21, B

This road on the south bank of the Tweed shares much of the history of its north bank partner. Stobie's 1770 map marks it as the road to Berwick, an indication perhaps that at that time it was the more popular of the two routes, avoiding Coldstream altogether. By crossing the river on the bridge at Kelso and using this road, the ford at Edenmouth could be avoided.

Its course took it through Sprouston, across the English border near Carham and on through the village of Wark to approach Cornhill from the south where it met the main road from Coldstream to Berwick and Newcastle.

Like its neighbour on the other bank, it was turnpiked in 1793, but the actual route was never altered in any way. Tolls were built at Sprouston and at the national boundary at Carham Burn.

Kelso to Berwick via Swinton (B6461) – Map 22, A

During the time of the great monasteries, large quantities of wool were taken from abbeys such as Kelso to Berwick for shipment abroad, which meant that a road of sorts must have existed between the two towns. Naturally every effort would have been made to avoid crossing difficult rivers and on this journey the only one would have been the Whiteadder shortly before reaching Berwick. Fortunately there was a normally shallow ford at what is now known as Canty's Brig and this was probably the chosen route. Nothing else is known about the rest of the way except that in the parish of Simprin (now incorporated into Swinton) the monks reputedly had a hospice or resting-house to ease the way. This could not have been all that far from the present road and it is interesting to conjecture that the routes at that time and today might not have been all that different.

With the loss of Berwick in 1482, the importance of this trade route would have gone. Even after the Union in 1603, trade through Berwick never really recovered and it would be many years before Border towns once more used Berwick for exporting. The road, or track, would have fallen into rapid disuse and much of it probably ceased to exist.

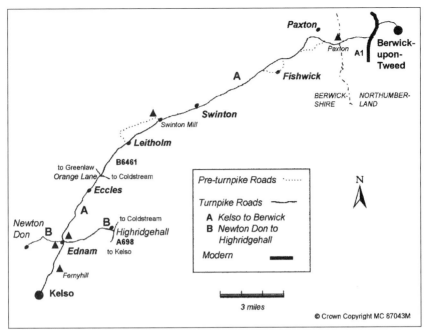

Map 22 – Kelso to Berwick; Newtown Don to Highridgehall.

The position changed in the 18th century with the agricultural revolution. The Merse of Berwickshire has the richest farmland in the Borders and a network or minor roads had been created through this area to enable people to have access to the various fields. In time, some of these became used by wheeled vehicles and out of them would have appeared the genesis of today's road pattern.

Armstrong's 1771 map of Berwickshire shows a road of sorts along this way, but it is difficult to comprehend it as a planned route; rather it appeared to be no more than a collection of connecting trackways. However, it did go through the same villages as it does at present – Ednam, Eccles, Leitholm, Swinton and close by Paxton before crossing the English border and into Berwick. The Turnpike Act of 1793 (an umbrella one to improve those roads around Kelso which had not been previously done) enabled work to start on upgrading these trackways into a proper road. From the Kelso end the road followed almost exactly that of the former minor ways as far as the approaches to Leitholm. Here the old road was straightened out, passing on the south side of Bughtrig instead of the north as before, then at Swinton Mill resumed the line of the former road into Swinton.

From Swinton, the ways coincided as far as a point about a mile west of Fishwick. The original road went through the settlement there, then made straight past Paxton House towards the English border. The turnpike road went to the north of Fishwick and made a detour to avoid the grounds of Paxton House. At the border, authority passed to another trust to take the road into Berwick, joining the road from Duns just before the town. Apart from alterations when the Berwick bypass was built in 1984, the route is virtually unchanged since the creation of the turnpike.

There were at least three tollhouses within a few miles of leaving Kelso, one at Fernyhill corner and two within the village of Ednam. It is unusual to find so many within close proximity of one another within one county and there was either the possibility that they were not all in use at any one time or, perhaps more likely, some of them were designed to cater for traffic using some of the side roads. The next one was at Swinton Mill cross-roads and the last at the national boundary near Paxton.

Newton Don to Highridgehall (unclassified) – Map 22, B

The cost of turnpiking this short cross-country road must have been very hard to justify and today it does appear strange that it should ever have been done at all. It appeared in a detailed 1839 map of turnpike roads in the Kelso area and started opposite Newton Don estate on the Stichill road (which would have been a much more suitable choice for turnpiking) and made its unremarkable way eastwards to Newtonlees Farm and Ednam. Here it crossed over the Kelso to Berwick road and continued on to meet the one to Coldstream near Highridgehall Farm. Perhaps this was why there were two tolls in Ednam, although how even one on this short turnpike could ever have been warranted is a mystery.

Kelso to Wooler and the south via Hadden Rig (B6352 and B6396, leading to A697) – Map 23, A

In chapter 10 reference is made to the Turnpike Act of 1765 which dealt with the way from Lauder through Kelso to the Border at the March Burn. There were more than one March Burn, for all the term meant was a burn marking part of the boundary between Scotland and England, but this specific one is now known as the Pressen Burn and lies seven miles east of Kelso.

The turnpike road followed the general route of an old trackway which crossed the ridge known as Hadden Rig, the scene of one of the last of the Border battles in 1542 between the Scots and the English. However the exit from Kelso was changed; previously it followed the south bank of the Tweed as far as Mellendean then turned up the hill near Easter Softlaw. The new road left the one to Hawick at Maxwellheugh and continued on what was to become the road to Yetholm for about one and a half miles before turning towards Easter Softlaw to rejoin the old road.

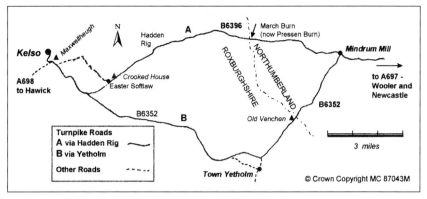

Map 23 – Kelso to Wooler and Newcastle.

In England the road followed the valley of the Bowmont Water through Mindrum Mill, Kilham and Kirknewton to join the main Coldstream to Wooler road at Akeld.

What the trustees were seeking was an alternative to the Coldstream route to Wooler, Newcastle and the south to carry the ever-increasing numbers of private carriages and post-chaises appearing on the road. With the opening of the Kelso Bridge in 1754 and the growth of decent inns in the town, they felt that they were approaching the dawn of a great age with the town becoming the hub of the carriage trade within the Borders. This did eventually happen but not at that time, for this route to England was never a popular one with coachmen and even the incentive of the 1769 purpose-built coaching inn known as the Cross Keys did little to help then. When stagecoaches started to operate through the Borders, none of them ever went by Hadden Rig, the operators preferring the well-tried Coldstream alternative. But Kelso did not lose out, for as will be shown in chapter 21, crack coaches to and from London (stage and mail) passed through the town from 1815 onwards, but none of them ever crossed the Tweed at the town, all did so at Coldstream.

Apart from Maxwellheugh, the only other toll before the border was at Crooked House near Easter Softlaw. Perhaps because of the lack of traffic, the Trustees had considerable difficulty in letting Crooked House; in 1840 it remained vacant and in 1854 the rent was reduced from £69 to £44 in an endeavour to find a tenant. Shortly after that, it disappeared from the list of tolls, indicating that it had been closed down.

Kelso to Wooler and the South via Town Yetholm
(B6352, leading to A697) – *Map 23, B*

This was another road created from trackways by the 1793 Kelso Turnpike Act. Although the need for an alternative route to Wooler is not at all clear, perhaps it was an attempt by the trustees to find a more popular way to the south so that Kelso could benefit from the lucrative trade being lost to the Coldstream road. Unfortunately, coach drivers and operators could not be persuaded to use it to any greater extent than the other one.

The new turnpike made use of an ancient track to Yetholm, sharing the first section out of Kelso with the Hadden Rig road. Just over a mile before Town Yetholm, the turnpike left the main track and took a parallel one past Cherrytrees, so did not actually enter the village at all. This may appear to have been a strange decision as it would cost nothing more to have gone through it, but the Trustees probably saw that the reason for the new road was not so much to serve the local community but to achieve a quick passage into England. At no time then did Town Yetholm ever have a turnpike road running through it and today's road into the village was no more than a track until late in the last century.

The road from Yetholm to Kelso at Maxwellheugh in 1810. In the background is Floors Castle before major structural alterations were made thirty years later. (from an engraving)

When the Bowmont valley was reached, the road followed the left bank with only a short journey to the Northumberland border. From there it continued to Mindrum Mill where it met and joined the Hadden Rig turnpike.

The tolls were at Kelso (Maxwellheugh) and close to the border. The latter was originally called Town Yetholm Mains or even Yetholm Mains, causing great confusion with Kirk Yetholm Mains Toll less than half a mile away across the Bowmont, so that it was not long before it was changed to Old Venchen. However even in the middle of the 19th century, the clerks writing the minutes of the Meeting of Kelso Trustees continued to use these names indiscriminately.

Kalemouth to Kirk Yetholm and the Border (B6401 and unclassified) – *Map 24*

This turnpike may have been created to make a reasonable road to connect Jedburgh with Wooler. There was an old track to Yetholm which led due east out of Jedburgh to Crailing Hall (an unclassified road follows this part of the route today) then went north-eastwards through Upper Crailing (now completely gone) and over Cessford Moor to Cessford and on to the village of Morebattle. The way then followed the existing road to Town Yetholm and neighbouring Kirk Yetholm and continued by the right bank of the Bowmont Water to the border.

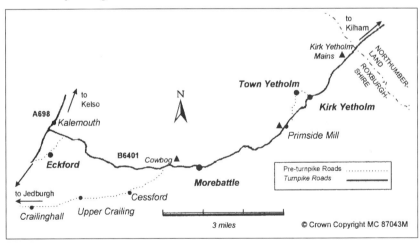

Map 24 – Kalemouth to Kirk Yetholm and the Border.

It was probably decided that a new turnpike all the way from Jedburgh would not have been justified through such a sparsely populated area, so the maximum use would have been made of the existing turnpike from Jedburgh to Kelso (the 'Great Road' to quote the trustees). There had been a trackway of sorts connecting Eckford with the Yetholms along the valley of the Kale Water and much of this was used, except that a new start was made at Kalemouth instead of going through Eckford village. From Morebattle the old way was taken as far as a point immediately past Primside Mill, then something rather strange happened. Instead of going to Town Yetholm as the old way had done, the new road veered off to the right near Duncanhaugh and made its way directly to Kirk Yetholm. Why Town Yetholm should have been bypassed is odd in itself, but to take the new road through a boggy haugh (which still floods today) seems to have been most illogical. This particular section no longer exists other than as a footpath, but in the 1839 turnpike map it is clearly shown. By 1863 however, all but the first few yards had gone from the first six-inch Ordnance Survey map, leaving only a footpath marked 'liable to floods'. By then the main road went through Town Yetholm as it continues to do today.

From Kirk Yetholm the road to the border ran parallel to the other turnpike along the Bowmont valley – but on the other side. In England the road was (and still is) even narrower than on the Scottish side and it is doubted whether many carriages ever used it. It followed the edge of the Cheviots to join the road from Kelso and Town Yetholm at Kilham.

The old toll house first known as Shotton Burn then as Kirk Yetholm Mains, on the unclassified road to Wooler close to the English border.

The date of this turnpike is not known, but by deduction it would have been after 1799 (when the Morebattle minister said that 'there were no turnpikes in this parish and the roads through it were very far from good and often impassable') and before the first reference to tolls on the road in 1823.

The tolls were at Cowbog west of Morebattle, Primside Mill and close by the border near today's Yetholm Mains. When the border toll was opened, it was called Shotton Burn, but later became Kirk Yetholm Mains after the local farm. Comment has already been made about the confusion this caused with the toll on the other side of the Bowmont. Even as late as 1872, mentions were made in the Trustee Minutes to Yetholm Mains, Kirk Yetholm Mains and Shotton Burn within two months of one another and all referring to this toll.

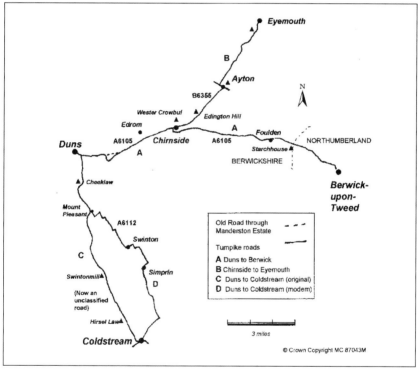

Map 25 – Duns to Berwick; Chirnside to Eyemouth and Duns to Coldstream.

Duns to Berwick (A6105) – *Map 25, A*

This way was well-established by 1770, going by way of Chirnside and Foulden before crossing into England. Until 1733 the road had gone straight through what was to become the Manderston estate to the east of Duns but In that year the road was moved round the southern perimeter where it has remained ever since. No directional changes were made when the road was turnpiked in 1792. Even today few changes have occurred other than the bypassing of Chirnside for through traffic.

There were tolls at Chirnside (Wester Crowbul) and at Starchhouse on the English border east of Foulden.

Chirnside to Eyemouth (B6355) – Map 25, B

This road was in existence by the late 18th century and the fact that there were tolls along its route indicates that it had been turnpiked at one time, but no records pertaining to this have been traced. At Ayton, it crossed over the Great North Road, then followed the Eye Water for the short journey into the port of Eyemouth.

The tolls were at Edington Hill east of Chirnside, Ayton and at Eyemouth just before entering the town.

Duns to Coldstream (A6112) – Map 25, C and D

This road was turnpiked in 1792, but with no apparent change to its direction at that time. It led south from Duns to Mount Pleasant and from there on to Swinton Mill and Coldstream. The latter part of the road was so straight (a rarity in Berwickshire) that people could be excused for thinking that the Romans played a part in the making of it.

It cannot be denied that it might have been too narrow for present-day traffic, but the solution reached in the 1960s was anything but satisfactory. What the Transport Department of the Scottish Office did was to declassify this road and substitute for it a tortuous route of existing minor roads south of Mount Pleasant through the village of Swinton and the settlement at Simprin to approach Coldstream along the river from the north-east. The previous road had entered Coldstream in the middle of the town.

The remarkable thing about the new way is that although some widening was carried out, no alterations were made to the great number of sharp bends along its length, each a reminder that the earliest roads in agricultural areas tended to follow the boundaries of individual fields.

On the old road there were tolls at Cheeklaw to the south of Duns, Swinton Mill and Hirsel Law at the north-east corner of the Hirsel Estate at Coldstream.

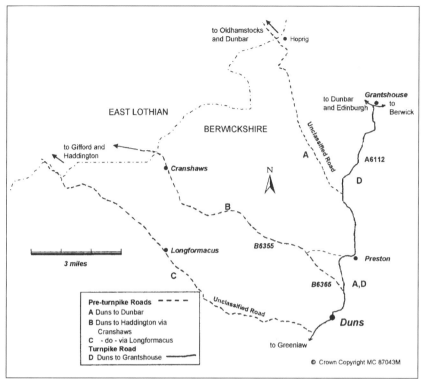

Map 26 – Duns to Grantshouse; Duns to Gifford.

Duns to Grantshouse (A6112) – *Map 26, A and D*

From Duns the original road went through the village of Preston then north and
north-westwards across moorland and past Hoprig to the county boundary. From
there it went to Oldhamstocks in East Lothian on its way to Dunbar. All the way
still exists as minor unclassified roads.

The new road built in the 1840s used the same road as far as a point some three
miles north of Preston, from where it ran north-eastwards to join the Great North
Road at Grantshouse. Neither section ever had tollhouses installed.

Duns to Gifford and Haddington (B6365 then B6355) – *Map 26, B and C*

In a Melrose Charter of 1227 reference was made to a way connecting Duns with
Haddington and known as *Ricardisrode* - 'Richard's Road'. Today there are two
roads out of Duns in this direction, although both come together as one shortly

after crossing into East Lothian. The first, the only classified one of the two, leaves Duns on the A6112 Grantshouse road before branching off to the left before Preston to follow part of the upper Whitadder Water to Cranshaws. Shortly after, the East Lothian border is crossed at the Whitadder Reservoir.

The second road starts from the opposite end of Duns, leaving the Greenlaw road at Clockmill and runs roughly parallel to the other one. It passes the Lammermuir village of Longformacus before crossing those hills at 1325 feet and descending into East Lothian. Despite being an unclassified road today, it was the only one shown in Armstrong's map of 1771 and could well have been Richard's Road. Neither road had ever been turnpiked.

Chapter 17

The Roadmakers –
Telford and McAdam

Thomas Telford

Although Telford cannot be claimed as a Borderer in the context of the area covered by this book, nonetheless he was born in 1757 at Westerkirk near Langholm in Dumfriesshire, only three miles from the Roxburghshire boundary. The son of an upland shepherd, he was apprenticed to an Edinburgh stonemason at the age of fifteen and employed for a number of years in the building of the New Town taking shape to the north of the appropriately-named Auld Reekie.

In 1793 he secured his first engineering appointment for the construction of the Ellesmere Canal, where he was required to design and build a large aqueduct. This brought almost immediate success and his fame as one of the premier civil engineers of the industrial revolution meant that he was always in demand. He was commissioned to report on the likely needs for civil engineering works in the Highlands of Scotland, arising from which he was appointed engineer for the Caledonian Canal and for the equally formidable task of making over 900 miles of new roads through treacherous country. From there he spent some time in southern Scotland and Wales surveying roads. Later work took him on drainage construction work in the Fens, the building of many bridges up and down the country and a number of dock and harbour projects. In 1827 he was elected a Fellow of the Royal Society and, in the following year the first President of the Institution of Civil Engineers. He died in London on 2nd September 1834.

Thomas Telford is best remembered as a brilliant civil engineer and many of his finest works proudly stand today as memorials to his genius: the Menai Bridge and Pontcysylte Aqueduct in Wales and the Caledonian Canal through the Great Glen. Some of his finest bridges are in Scotland: across the Tay at Perth, the Clyde at Glasgow, the Dean Bridge in Edinburgh and the Spey Bridge at Craigellachie. As far as is known, there are no existing examples of his bridges within the Borders, yet he figured prominently in all the bustle of the 1820s when road improvements were taking place to cope with the ever-increasing demands made by users.

Using engineering principles in place of the haphazard methods common at that time, he insisted on careful drainage, both underneath the roadway and the adjoining strips of land, so diminishing the risks of washaways and landslips which were constant problems. He also required the most careful grading of stones for the foundation and the surface, using uniformly sized large stones for the former and irregular but small stones for the latter. Before, builders had attempted to bind the foundations and surface with clay – with dreadful results. As the impact of the horses and the iron tyres of the carriages and wagons gradually broke down the corners of the small stones, the resultant dust worked into the structure of the road, hardening and binding into a smooth and virtually watertight covering. He was careful to ensure that his roads were cambered to throw water off, something which had not been done since the Romans left.

This expertise was put to good use throughout the country, including the Scottish Borders, but Telford had another important function to perform; that of the road surveyor. Authorities were coming to grips with the problems of highways having gradients which were quite unsuitable for coach and carriage traffic. Steep hills could just be tackled by men on horseback and strings of pack-animals, but the difficulties of coping with precipitous uphill climbs and the dangers of overturning a carriage or, perhaps even worse, having to deal with runaways on steep downhill sections, made the lives of coach drivers and their passengers anything but easy.

In the Borders, he carried out a number of major surveys, all meticulously done, showing his ideas for the improvement of existing roads and, in some cases, completely new ones as well. All these roads were connected with the London to Edinburgh routes at the instigation of the General Post Office, coach operators, heritors or turnpike trustees; parties all concerned with road improvements although from different angles. The Post Office wanted the cheapest, fastest and most efficient way to carry mails between the two capitals, as did the coach operators for their passengers, whereas the heritors and trustees wanted their particular road or roads to be better than other routes so that the Post Office and coach proprietors could be convinced that it was the only feasible way to go.

Two surveys were made in 1820, the first being Telford's ideas for a completely new route from Edinburgh to Yorkshire, known as the Aldstone Moor Line. The existing road from Edinburgh to Hawick would be used, then a new road would be built over or close to the old way to Newcastleton. From there would be a completely new way over the moors east of Carlisle to Brampton in Cumberland and across the Pennines to Catterick Bridge to connect with the Great North Road there. Nothing came of this adventurous plan.

The other survey of that year was made so that the route through Hexham to Catterick in Yorkshire could be considered for a mailcoach service. Much of this way is now the A68 from Edinburgh through Jedburgh and Corbridge to Darlington, but at that time most of it south of Otterburn consisted of the remains of Roman

Dere Street. This route was rejected by the authorities. In their report, they commented unfavourably on the deep valleys along the way and to the crossing over the Cheviots at Carter Fell, '*so although Hexham and Jedburgh appear in a strait* (sic) *direction on the map, yet in execution, this line would only admit of a crooked and imperfect road, with a very high summit at 1416 feet'*. It would appear that Telford was never asked to propose any improvements to this road, yet by 1830, coaches were travelling this way as far as Otterburn before going east to Newcastle.

In 1822 Telford made a thorough survey of what was referred to as the Wooler-Coldstream Line connecting Yorkshire with Scotland. Here his report has been preserved in the archives of the Institution of Civil Engineers in London together with the plans showing in great detail his proposed alterations to existing roads along the way, including the most radical one to bypass Coldstream altogether as described in Chapter 8.

Due to the costs involved however, few of his proposals for this road were ever accepted, notable exceptions being the route alteration over the Lammermuirs at Soutra and the bypassing of Norton and Drummonds Hall south of Carfraemill, both being carried out shortly afterwards.

In 1823, Telford carried out a survey of the Great North Road between Morpeth and Edinburgh, again at the instigation of the General Post Office, with proposals for improvements. As far as can be ascertained, none of these was ever carried out, but it did give the authorities ammunition in the battle of the mailcoach routes which, like so many other cases, finished in a compromise. The following year, apparently as a result of Telford's findings, the new night Mailcoach was routed via Kelso and Coldstream, although the day Mail continued on the Great North Road through Berwick.

During a four-year period from 1824, he made surveys of the Edinburgh to Carlisle road through Hawick. Little is known about this work, but perhaps it was he who suggested the direct connection between Galashiels and Selkirk which was completed in 1832.

One further survey carried out by Telford in the Borders was for a railway between Glasgow and Berwick via the valleys of the Clyde and Tweed. This was in 1810 before steam locomotion was a possibility and what he proposed was a double line with stone sleepers to take small trucks drawn by horses. The cost was estimated at £368,000; the proposal failed to elicit sufficient support and was dropped. Even with the railway mania of the 19th century, no serious attempt was ever made to plan a direct link between Glasgow and Berwick through the Tweed Valley.

The poet Southey, a close friend of Telford, used to describe him as *The Colossus of Roads*, a title which somehow was later passed on to McAdam.

To the end of his life Telford, normally a man of vision, failed to grasp the significance of the emerging age of steam, preferring to stand by the canal system which he had done so much to develop.

John Loudon McAdam

McAdam (or sometimes Macadam) was born at Ayr in 1756, one year before Telford. He emigrated to America at the age of fourteen to work for an uncle there and obviously did very well, for on his return to Scotland he bought an estate at Sauchie near Maybole. On this estate he began experimenting with road materials, the workable results of which led him to achieve great fame throughout Britain and further afield as one of the finest road engineers, with the added kudos of having had a civil engineering process named after him.

Many of his basic ideas for improving road surfaces followed closely on those put forward by Telford and it is known that the two had met on a number of occasions. With two such strong characters coming together, it was perhaps inevitable that professional rivalry sometimes developed into distrust and animosity.

McAdam went further into the materials being used for road-making. He agreed with Telford's dictum that there should be larger stones at the foundation level, with diminishing sizes towards the surface, but had the novel idea of breaking the stones before laying them. Rounded stones from alluvial deposits or even river-beds were the commonest source of supply for road-making and McAdam found that they would bed down much better and tend not to move about if they were first broken. This apparently simple idea and the improved roads which stemmed from it was the major reason for his later fame and soon a *macadamised* road was one built in this fashion. He was very strict to ensure that the correct size of stone was being used. In a report to one committee he said '*I always make my surveyors carry a pair of scales and a six ounce weight in their pocket and when they come to a heap of stones, they weigh one or two of the largest*'. Stone-breaking was now a new rural occupation and it was a common sight to see workmen by the roadsides busily preparing piles of materials with the aid of a small hammer.

After McAdam's time, when gas production was becoming popular in most towns, tar was a by-product and it was found that by adding this to the highway surface, a watertight and long-lasting roadway was created. Today this is the basis for most sealed roads everywhere in the world, universally referred to as *tarmacadam* or simply *tarmac*.

Compared with Telford, McAdam's involvement in the Borders was small, but he did advise turnpike trustees on several improvements to their roads. The best documented was his proposal for the Jedburgh road which has been dealt with in chapter 9. He spent more time in Midlothian, however. Further south, he secured many lucrative posts, perhaps the grandest of these being 'Surveyor General of the Metropolitan Roads' with an award of £10,000. It was on one of his few later trips to Scotland that he died suddenly in 1836 whilst supervising survey work for a new road near Moffat. In his lifetime, it has been estimated that he surveyed over 30,000 miles of roads throughout Britain.

Part II

Early Road Transport in the Scottish Borders

An early stagecoach similar to those in use about 1800 between Edinburgh and Selkirk, Jedburgh and Kelso. *(from a title page in the 1897 Victoria Edition of 'The Antiquary' by Sir Walter Scott)*

Chapter 18

Early Road Transport

It is not known when the first wheeled vehicles arrived in the Borders, although it was likely that at the time of the Roman occupation the Celtic tribes were already familiar with them. These may have been the means by which materials were carried around their homelands, but their most important use would have been as war chariots in their constant battles and skirmishes with neighbouring tribes and the Roman invaders.

Road vehicles were extensively used by the Romans and an essential element of their speedy advances into the far north of Britain. They were the reason for the superior types of road they built; roads that could withstand the constant erosion caused by carts and wagons.

In the long dark ages after the Romans left, little is known of any forms of wheeled road transport and it may not have been until the 12th century that they were once again brought into use, particularly by the Angles who had gradually displaced the Celts in the Borders and were in turn to be dominated by the Norman overlords. The abbeys of Melrose, Kelso, Jedburgh and Dryburgh derived considerable incomes from the flourishing sheep industry and the wool and skins for export to Flanders were shipped through Scotland's largest seaport at Berwick. As mentioned in Chapter 3, much of these exports would have been carried by long strings of pack-horses or mules, although it is known that primitive carts of a sort had also been used.

Long after the monasteries and the lucrative wool trade had gone, the pack-horses would have been the only major carriers of bulk materials and until the 18th century, most coal, lime and other supplies to the Borders had to be taken in this way. Each carried trussed-up bundles on either side, suspended from a primitive harness, to provide some balance to the usually overloaded animals. Trains of pack-animals required little in the way of roads and it was easy for them to be deviated in times of flooding.

Merchandise was sometimes carried on horseback to supply the small shops in the Border towns, but much of the domestic trade would have been conducted by the packmen or pedlars who made their way from house to house with their limited assortment of small luxuries and wares the people could not readily make for themselves.

Carriers

In Chapter 4 it was shown the effect that changes in agriculture had on the people of the Borders and indeed the rest of the country in the early part of the 18th century. With these changes came the need for much better roads; ones with surfaces and gradients capable of taking loaded wheeled vehicles.

At first these vehicles were primitive unsprung wagons pulled by teams of oxen, horses or mules, and used by the growing band of carriers who made a business of taking goods on behalf of others. Almost every town had at least one licensed carrier who often ran reasonably regular services between his home base and the nearest large centres such as Edinburgh and Newcastle. Inns in the large towns were the usual gathering-places for these carriers and these were where bargaining took place to secure a return load.

In time, people wanting to send goods into the countryside knew that the appropriate carrier would be at a certain inn on a certain day. Often these carriers made an additional income by leaving a little space on either side of the wagon so that passengers could also be carried. These were travellers with just sufficient money to pay the modest fare and so were able to avoid the alternative of a long walk. But the wretches had to sit out in all weathers with their legs dangling over the side as the wagons made their slow progress over indifferent roads and across fords. So these cumbersome vehicles became the first form of public transport and they endured in the Borders until the arrival of the railways in the late 1840s.

It was the carriers who imported the coal and lime from the Lothians and North Northumberland and all the basic farm materials to meet the agricultural challenge. Similarly, they took the farming produce to the enlarging industrial markets in Glasgow and England as well as the rapidly-increasing population of Edinburgh. This marked the re-emergence of the Borders as a major agricultural producer at a time when the industrial revolution was creating demands to feed the newly-arrived workers.

Some carriers had atrocious road conditions to contend with, even after the roads had come under the control of turnpike trusts. In 1770 the Selkirk carrier took two weeks to go from there to Edinburgh carrying a load of six hundredweight at a time. This might have been the same carrier who, during the summer months and when the weather was dry, found it preferable to drive along the channels of the Gala Water rather than the road which ran roughly parallel to the river. Presumably some improvements were made before the first stagecoaches ran that way some years later.

The carrier's wagons carried considerable weight and it appears that the narrowness of the wheel rims and lack of springing caused much trouble with many of the turnpike road trustees. Ruts were often one foot deep and it was not long before there were demands for legislation to restrict wagons on the roads to those fitted with wheels with rims at least 16 inches wide, so turning them into small road-rollers. This caused great uproar amongst the ranks of the carriers, who protested that not only would they be burdened by such cumbersome wheels, but they would be maintaining roads so that pleasure carriages could have a smoother ride. Nothing appeared in the statute books on this matter, but several people drew up plans for such types of wagons, one of them Daniel Bourn in 1763 who produced drawings of a 'newly Invented Wagon', but it is not known whether any of these found their way into the Borders.

Private Carriages

The first carriages were essentially developments of the basic design for wagons – front and rear axles connected by a long wooden pole, at that time called a perch. The first real improvement was the introduction of springing, at first by the use of leather braces to support the body of the carriage and later, towards the end of the 18th century, by steel springs. When elliptic springs were used early the following century, a turning point came with carriage design, for then it became possible to dispense with the perch, making for lighter and more elegant vehicles.

A post-chaise of the late 18th century of the type used by most coaching inns for hiring out complete with horses and driver.

From about 1730 onwards, the better-off had a variety of options for getting about, all based of course on the use of horses. The richest could travel in their own carriages, either drawn by their own horses or specially hired so that they could be changed at post-houses on a long journey. The less well-endowed could hire a post-chaise and horses which increasingly became available at inns and post-houses up and down the country.

Privately-owned carriages came in many forms and until the arrival of the railways and later the motor car, they became very sophisticated status symbols, with wealthy neighbours vying with one another. The choice of carriage became bewildering, with very exuberant names to describe their shape and use. Single-horse carriages usually had two wheels and names such as whiskeys, cabriolets, buggies and gigs, each differing in a subtle way. Similarly, with the four-wheeled carriages pulled by two or more horses there was a number of names such town-coach (almost identical to a stagecoach), brougham, chariot, landau, barouche, fourgon, drag and phaeton (a light open carriage often referred to as a 'high flyer'). A hybrid of the two was the fashionable curricle which had two wheels but was drawn by a pair of horses abreast on either side of a pole. However unlikely it sounds now, a curricle was used by the Post Office in the 1830s for running a fast mail service between Edinburgh and Newcastle by Coldstream to augment the mailcoach on the Great North Road.

Sometimes confusion is caused by the expressions *coaches* and *carriages*. They are often used synonymously and there is really little to choose between them, but it is generally accepted that although carriages may be open or closed, coaches are always closed vehicles.

Wheeled transport could only be used on improved roads, either turnpike or 'statute', and for this reason some parts of the Borders had to wait a long time until wheels came to them. In remote places like the valleys of the Ettrick, Yarrow, Manor and Bowmont, the only vehicles ever encountered were simple sledges which travelled with difficulty on what passed for roads. In the NSA for Ettrick in the 1830s, the writer mentioned that there were 30 miles of road in the parish on which any carriage could travel. '*I remember*' says an old man of 80, '*when there was not a cart in the parish, not above Singlee*'. He went on to say that now there were 36.

Early Coaches

Long before the first of the Border roads were turnpiked, attempts had been made to run coaches on the Great North Road through Berwickshire, so connecting Edinburgh and London by something better than going on horseback or risking a perilous journey by sea. But all attempts seemed to have failed. Horrendous road surfaces, lack of facilities on the way and poorly designed coaches were all too much.

As early as 1657 coaches were advertised to go from London to various places including Edinburgh once every three weeks for £4.10s., in all cases with good coaches and fresh horses on the roads. There is no record of any of these coaches ever having crossed the Scottish border and this may be borne out by the fact that the following year an advertisement for coach services from London made no reference to Edinburgh nor indeed anywhere north of York. Even by 1662 there were only six stage coaches in England and none in Scotland.

Nothing more is heard about ventures into Scotland until an advertisement of 30th October 1727 informed the public that

> *'whosoever wants the Stage Coach for London may enquire at Mr. Clark, vintner, over against the Earl of Murray's lodgings in Canongate, Edinburgh, where they will be furnished with good coaches and horses (beside the stage coach) for £30 from Edinburgh to London on seven days advertisement by the said Mr.Clark.....'*

The next year, the following appeared on 13th August:

> *'..... set out from London to Edinburgh upon the 5th inst, a handsome and convenient coach and six, containing nine passengers and being expected in Edinburgh on the 18th, will set out for London on the 21st or 22nd, enquire at John Somerville's, gunsmith, Canongate.'*

The first advertisement rather gives the impression that the £30 quoted was for the hire of the entire coach and this may have been quite a common occurrence in those days, but even so the cost was very high indeed by later standards and would have limited its use to the very rich. What is particularly interesting is the reference to a stagecoach, despite the fact that no Edinburgh newspaper in that year carried any advertisement for one. The second coach could have been either a stage or a hired coach and the thirteen days anticipated for the journey appears a lot more realistic than the optimistic seven days quoted in the first. Again though, there is little or no evidence to indicate any degree of success in the venture.

For a few years, various announcements were made, including references to the fact that the stagecoach '*continues to go from Canongate to London*' but it is strange that there appears to be no other contemporary references to this mysterious stagecoach. It was not until 1754 that something more definite appeared when the *Edinburgh Evening Courant* carried this advertisement:

> '*The Edinburgh stage coach for the better accommodation of passengers, will be altered to a new genteel two-end glass machine, hung on steel springs, exceeding light and easy, to go in ten days in summer and twelve in winter, and to set out the first Tuesday in March, and continue it from Hosea Eastgates, the Coach and Horses in Dean Street, Soho, London, and from John Somerville's in the Canongate, Edinburgh, every other Tuesday and meet at Burrough Bridge on Saturday, and set out from thence on Monday morning, and get to London and Edinburgh on Friday. In the winter to set out from London and Edinburgh every other Monday morning, and to go to Burrough Bridge on Saturday night, and to set out from thence on Monday morning and get to London and Edinburgh on Saturday night. Passengers to pay as usual. Performed, if God permits, by your dutiful servant, Hosea Eastgate. Care is taken of small parcels according to their value.*'

This is the first clear indication of a regular service between the capitals and proved to be the precursor of all future such services, all of which passed through the Borders by at least four separate routes. The first daily service from London into Scotland started in 1779 and this did not go to Edinburgh but to Glasgow by way of Carlisle. It was not until 1786 that Edinburgh also had the benefit of a daily London service, although this was not a stagecoach (or a *diligence* as it was often referred to), but the newest innovation on Scottish roads – a mailcoach. In dealing with stagecoaches, services that are termed daily never ran on Sundays, whereas *daily* mailcoaches actually ran on every day of the week. The post office was the only organisation ever to be successful in running Sunday services.

Thomas Somerville (a Jedburgh minister) in his '*Life and Times*' gives a fascinating account of a journey between London and Edinburgh in 1769. Looking for some means of getting there, he met someone who offered him a free and safe conveyance to Edinburgh, although there were strings attached. He was to take custody of a valuable parcel and when he duly arrived at the coach which had been specially prepared, he was handed a pair of loaded pistols with a list of instructions for the journey. The 'parcel' turned out to be a chest containing about ten thousand guineas destined for the old Bank of Scotland, an enormous amount then and today equivalent to well over one million pounds. In the instructions, he was required to write daily to addresses in Edinburgh and London, make only a short stop at each stage, not to travel after 8pm, not to lodge in the larger towns and never to lose sight of the package which had to be deposited in his bedroom behind a locked door. Its weight meant that it required two porters to move it from one carriage to another and the landlords cursed at the load which endangered the bottom of their carriages. He remarked that his journey was by no means an agreeable one, but despite his misapprehension, he arrived safely in Edinburgh and handed the package over to Mr. Innes, the cashier of the bank.

This journey seems to have taken only four days in May of that year, a remarkably quick time compared with other coaches, but it should be remembered that for security reasons, very little time was spent at posting-houses along the way. One thing which becomes clear is that different coaches were used for each stage of the journey, indicating that through coaches were not common then. In addition, it is interesting that even at this early stage of coaching development these posting-houses were sufficiently well equipped to let the minister have the required coach and horses. He gave a list of all these places with the distances between them and from Woollerhaughead (a posting-house south of Wooler) these were indicated as follows:

To Cornhill	14 miles
Greenlaw	12
Norton Moor	12
Blackshiels	10
Edinburgh	14
Total from London	**385 miles**

In 1785, just one year before the mailcoach, another daily service had started, this time to Newcastle. The recently completed turnpike road over Soutra was chosen, through Greenlaw and Coldstream to Wooler and Morpeth and it proved very popular. The advertisement is particularly interesting as it includes all kinds of detail:

'..... to run through in one day the Newcastle and Edinburgh Diligence, the proprietors of the Newcastle coach (by way of Wooler-haugh-head and Cornhill) in order to accommodate their friends and the public still better, have agreed to set out a Diligence every day (Sunday excepted) to carry three inside passengers easily - each to pay from Newcastle to Edinburgh £1.16s, allowed 14 lbs weight of luggage, all above to pay 2d. per pound for the whole distance or in proportion to the miles they go. Passengers taken up on the road to pay 4d. per mile. The above machine sets out at one o'clock the said mornings from Mr. Hugh Brodie's of the Turks Head Inn, Newcastle , and from James Robertson's the Black Bull Inn, Foot of Pleasance, Edinburgh. Have good convenience for luggage, parcels, boxes, &c., &c., which will be delivered on arrival. The proprietors will not be accountable for any parcel, box &c. above the value of £5 on any consideration whatsoever and those that send goods must observe to pack them sufficient to undergo the friction of the carriage, otherwise the proprietors will not be answerable for the consequences.'

The advertisement went on to show a list of the inn proprietors along the way where horses were changed, then finished with details of a connection which could be made at Newcastle for the onward journey to London. A through fare from Edinburgh to London was quoted at £5.7s.

By the end of the 18th century, the 1785 service seems to have been replaced by one going all the way to London. It was the first Scottish coach to be given a name. The *'Royal Charlotte'* (taking the name of George III's queen) ran on Mondays, Wednesdays and Fridays from the Black Bull at the head of Leith Walk at 5am and the fare for the entire journey was £7 7s. Described as a light post coach, it went, like its predecessor, by Soutra, Greenlaw and Coldstream.

The decision to take this important service by way of Soutra was prompted by the poor state of the Great North Road, despite the Pease Bridge nearing completion, and it had far-reaching effects. Innkeepers and other interested parties along the Berwick road were not slow to complain about the valuable custom which was taken away from them and the turnpike trustees were equally concerned as clearly toll revenue would be affected. This in time led to radical improvements along the way of the coastal road, reinforced by considerable pressure from the Post Office, but for the closing years of the 18th century, the stagecoaches went by Souta although the mailcoaches continued to use the Great North Road as they had done from the beginning.

The 18th century closed with few Borderers enjoying stagecoach services run for their benefit. They could take advantage of the cross-border coaches, provided they could make their way by some other means to the nearest stage. All this would soon change.

Coaching Inns

Unlike England, Scotland does not have a long history of wayside inns. An Englishman, Fynes Moryson, who travelled from Berwick to Stirling in 1598, observed that he *'did never see nor heare that they* (The Scots) *have any publike Innes with signs hanging out, but the better sort of citizens will entertain passengers upon acquaintance or entreaty"*. This was to change with the prospect of coach travel, which would never have been possible had it not been for inns along the roads on which they would pass. Most of the early ones had modest beginnings (probably as simple wayside inns) providing basic board and lodgings for travellers and facilities for stabling and feeding horses. Within a short time, some of them started to hire out a simple coach known as a post-chaise to supply a form of early taxi service. Horses were provided, as was a driver, usually referred to as a 'boy'. These 'boys' were nearly always grown men, often verging on the elderly and tended to be dressed in a uniform way with a red jacket, breeches, short top-boots and a large beaver hat. Other services offered by these inns were the hiring of horses to pull one's own carriage and the hiring of riding horses. Most of these facilities were provided essentially to advertise the particular inn and so attract custom.

At first known as posting-houses, they were usually from about ten to fifteen miles apart depending on the terrain, so providing suitable places for changing horses. A number of them would remain in business into the 20th century to become roadside hotels. When stagecoaches started to run, many of these inns were extended to take advantage of this business as well and they then described themselves as coaching inns . Most of the first stagecoach services were operated by the proprietors of these inns and for some years they successfully competed in an enlarging market until the professional operators with their network of routes squeezed them out. In Kelso, for example, The Cross Keys and The White Swan both ran stagecoach services to Edinburgh in competition with one another.

Naturally there had to be sufficient room for stabling the horses and storing the tackle and fodder and the necessary buildings for this were usually put behind the main structure. Access to the back was either by a passage at the side of the building (as can still be seen at the Black Bull in Lauder) or through a carriageway built into the main inn, as at the Cross Keys in Kelso. With recent building alterations, this carriageway is no longer obvious.

The well-known Black Bull Inn at Lauder, one of the busiest of the Borders coaching inns early in the 19th century. The stables were behind the building, with access through the opening on the right-hand side of the picture.

Chapter 19

Stagecoaches and Mailcoaches

Stagecoaches may be defined as public service vehicles designed specifically for the carriage of passengers, drawn by horses and running to a published timetable. At first the stated times were very approximate and usually quoted to the nearest half-hour, but later as reliability and competition increased, quarter-hours were normally used.

These coaches ran in stages (hence the name), usually being from ten to fifteen miles apart depending on the terrain and availability of facilities.

On local services, the driver was the sole crew-member who, during the journey, was responsible for time-keeping, the welfare of passengers and horses and dealing with minor or sometimes major repairs to the coach and harness. As soon as the next stage was reached, his duties ceased until such time as the next one started. At the stage, ostlers were responsible for changing and feeding the horses while servants from the inn were expected to load and offload the coach. This gave the drivers sufficient time to swagger about and take advantage of the admiration they enjoyed from bystanders of all ages. His uniform consisted of a broad-brimmed hat, a huge coloured neckerchief, a bright striped waistcoat and knee-breeches to meet his jockey-boots. For some curious reason, he always referred to the horses as *cattle*.

On the longer journeys (including London services), guards were also carried on stagecoaches, especially if the route was notorious for the activities of highwaymen.

At first, stagecoaches were usually owned and run by innkeepers, but gradually the professional operators (by means fair and foul) took over most of the routes so that by the heyday of the 1830s, a privately run stagecoach in the Borders was becoming a rarity.

Operating such a service required considerable administration, for sufficient horses had always to be available at the staging posts. A frequent service would arrange for their own horses to be stabled at the staging-inns and have agreed with the innkeeper regarding emergency replacements. A service running only once or twice a week (a common occurrence in the earlier years) could ill afford to have horses standing by idly, so they usually hired horses at the various inns on the way, often an unsatisfactory arrangement.

In the Borders, a typical local stagecoach service to Edinburgh from towns such as Jedburgh, Kelso and Duns went between forty and fifty miles. For a two-horse coach involving three changes en route, this meant the use of at least eight horses just to complete the journey. In the 1820s and 30s, with improved roads and more reliable coaches, many journeys to the capital could have a return journey on the same day, so that an additional two horses had to be available at Edinburgh to replace the tired pair which had just arrived. If, as was often the case, the coach was a four-in-hand, then the number of required horses had to be doubled.

Stagecoaches originally came in all shapes and sizes, the first of them being very clumsy ill-sprung vehicles often requiring at least six horses if the going was poor. Sir Walter Scott described a stagecoach as it would have been in 1755:

'covered with dull black leather, studded, by way of ornament with broad-headed nails, with oval windows with quarters, the frames painted red. On the panels were displayed, in large characters, the names of the places whence the coach started and whither it went. The roof rose on a high curve, with an iron rail around it. The coachman and guard sat in front upon a high narrow boot, often garnished with a spreading hammer-cloth with a deep fringe. Behind was an immense basket, supported by iron bars, in which passengers were carried at lower fares. The wheels were painted red. The whole coach was usually drawn by three horse, on the first of which a postillion rode with a cocked hat and a long green and gold coat. The machine groaned and creaked as it went along with every tug the horses gave, and the speed was frequently but four miles an hour.'

An early stagecoach showing the primitive suspension arrangement which must have made for a most uncomfortable journey.

From Scott's description, the coach referred to was probably a long-distance one, for local services in Scotland at that time scarcely existed and certainly the fact that it carried a guard is another clue. Postillions, who rode on the back of one of the leading horses, were rarely regularly used after about 1800 due to all sorts of improvements.

By 1830 coaches became much lighter and conformed more to a standard pattern. They were sturdy and handsome, built for endurance rather than comfort, the body containing a sparsely-upholstered compartment for six passengers, a boot at the back and front for their luggage and sometimes extra passengers and rough benches on the roof to take a further ten to twelve. The springs were now of steel instead of the stout leather used on earlier vehicles, but as before there were no means of braking apart from the skid-pan or shoe which hung on a chain underneath the body. The intention was when descending steep hills, or even attempting a sudden stop, skidding could be minimised if the skid-pan were slipped under the nearest wheel. Naturally this was a difficult job for the solo driver and most of them were loath to use it.

Such coaches took about six months to build and usually cost from £60 to £125 depending on the standard of finish. Private carriages of the same type could cost considerably more with better internal fittings and could rise to about £300. The timbers used were seasoned ash and oak, with mahogany for the panelling. The centre of the wheel was of elm with spokes of oak and rims of ash, all bound together with an iron hoop known as a tire. The roof and upper parts were covered in leather or fustian, a type of heavy durable cloth. The coaches were often gaudily coloured in the livery of the operators, needing up to 25 coats of paint and varnish to achieve the desired effect.

Unlike private carriages, the coach interiors were usually sparsely furnished and, according to one writer *'dirty, spartan and malodorous'*. Another was more kind:

'The inside of the coach is fitted up with spring cushions, and a reading lamp lighted with wax, for the accommodation of those who wish to amuse themselves on the road, the inside backs and seats are also fitted up with hair cushions, rendering them more comfortable to passengers than anything hitherto brought out in the annals of coaching. And to prevent frequent disputes respecting seats, every seat is numbered. Persons booking themselves at the office will receive a card with a number upon it, thereby doing away with the disagreeables that occur daily in the old style.'

The offices referred to were in the larger terminals such as Edinburgh, where the east end of Princes Street had at least three, operated on behalf of different coaching companies. They were often squalid affairs where few people would have wished to hang about and little else was done there apart from the sale of coach tickets. Outside the cities, tickets could sometimes be purchased at the inns where coaches stopped en route, but often this had to be obtained from the driver as he was the only one who knew what space was available on the vehicle. There appears to have been no facilities available for pre-booking at intermediate points, communication of course being the problem.

Mailcoaches

Whilst stagecoaches dealt primarily with passengers and carried very little freight other than luggage, mailcoaches were carriers of the Royal Mail and though they nearly always took passengers as well, they were of secondary importance. The two vehicles were basically similar in appearance but at first there was no provision for outside passengers on mailcoaches. Later, passengers on the mails were permitted to travel on top as well as inside , but generally the total number tended to be limited to six.

The coaches were not owned by the Post Office but were supplied and run under contract by operators who were often stagecoach proprietors and sometimes coach-builders as well. The contractor provided the drivers, but each coach carried a guard who was a Post Office employee and who was responsible for all the mails, including loading and off-loading the bags at intermediate stops. Originally mailcoaches did not have to meet toll charges, but in Scotland from 1813 they were required to pay like everyone else and it was the guard who had to settle with the tollhouse-keeper. He also had the task of ensuring that the published timetable was strictly adhered to, sometimes risking death or injury to get the mails through on time. In addition to these Post Office duties, he was expected to attend to the needs of passengers, helping them on and off with their luggage. He also kept the way-bill and time-bill, although the former was not onerous as the mails usually carried a limited number of passengers, most of them terminus to terminus. One dangerous job was to handle the skid-pan when this became necessary, a task normally done by the driver on stagecoaches. Finally, he was expected to make routine inspections of the wheels, axles and undercarriage at regular intervals.

Every year he was supplied with a new uniform of red coat, blue waistcoat and cockaded hat with gold lace. Before joining the coach, he was issued with a time-piece in a sealed box, a blunderbuss and a brace of pistols. In Edinburgh, before the starting point for mailcoaches was moved to Catherine Street at the top of Leith Walk, the guards used to muster outside the General Post Office, collect their bags and weapons then went up the hill on horseback or in chaises to the *Coach and Horses* at the top of the Canongate from where all the mailcoaches started.

The guards also carried a horn to warn of the imminent arrival of the mail and to ensure that tollkeepers were alerted. In the days before inflation was a meaningful word, his pay levels, like everyone else, hardly changed at all over the years.. It started at seven shillings and sixpence per week, rising to thirty shillings after 20 years.

Working for two masters created all sorts of trouble between the driver and the guard; the former suspecting that he was constantly being spied on and reported for the slightest misdemeanour, the latter feeling that he had so much more to do during the journey. There were probably faults on both sides, but the miracle was that despite this friction, the mailcoach services ran with an amazing punctuality record and were the envy of postal authorities throughout Europe.

Unlike stagecoaches, the mails had a standardised livery throughout Britain, this being blue and orange until the death of George III in 1820, after which the more sombre black and maroon was substituted. In both cases, the doors carried the Royal Crest, above which *Royal Mail* appeared together with the names of both terminals. The sides carried the insignia of the various Orders of Chivalry. These coaches were well maintained and were always spotlessly clean (on the outside anyway) when they left. With weather and road conditions, they would not have stayed in that condition for very long.

Unlike ordinary stagecoaches, great importance was attached to time-keeping; times were kept not to the quarter of an hour but to the minute and the Post Office jealously guarded their reputation in this regard. Lateness without reasonable excuse was a serious offence.

The contractor had to make all the same arrangements for horses as was the case with stagecoaches, frequently on a much larger scale. On the Edinburgh to London mail service, there were 28 changes for every journey, each coach needing 112 horses based on a team of four. With up to ten coaches in use at any one time, the total number of horses required was about 600. These horses had a short life on mail runs; for to ensure good timings, they were usually constantly and brutally whipped by the driver and it is recorded that in 1821 no less than eighteen horses dropped dead on the Great North Road. At that time the coach took 56 hours for the journey, achieving speeds of ten or eleven miles per hour in favourable stretches. Today it does seem incredible that horses had to suffer so much when a few hours or so over 400 miles would have made very little difference.

It is even worse to realise that sometimes the amount of mail actually carried between the capitals was quite small. A friend of Walter Scott remembered the days when the mail-bag came up with only one letter in it and none to go back. Edinburgh newspapers more than once reported the arrival of the *London post bearing no mails'*.

Mailcoaches and stagecoaches often ran in competition with one another and this led to a number of incidents, some of them with fatal results. Where a choice existed, most passengers would opt for the mailcoach despite the higher fares usually charged, for they always carried the extra benefit of the armed guard.

Coach hold-ups by highwaymen were rare in Scotland and virtually unknown in the Borders, the simple explanation being that services were so sparse that the thieves would have quickly tired of waiting for the next coach to come along. On the approaches to London the position was very different and this was the happy hunting grounds of people like Dick Turpin who made rich pickings on the busy roads.

The first mailcoach in Britain ran from London to Bristol in 1784, followed quickly by a network of services which included to Edinburgh via Berwick in 1786. Apart from the one introduced to Aberdeen from Edinburgh in 1798, there were no other mailcoach services in Scotland until after 1800. Later services south of Edinburgh and through the Borders were those to Dumfries in 1806 (to connect with the Irish Mail there) and to Carlisle the following year.

The Edinburgh postmaster announced that daily at 4pm starting on 27th November 1786, the first London mailcoach was to depart from Mr. Drysdale's, Cowgate Port, carrying bags for Haddington, Dunbar, Press, Dunse (off-loaded at Press) and Berwick. According to the Scots Magazine of that date, the coach was light and neat with four horses and took two and a half days, known as the 60 hour coach.

The following day, a large crowd gathered to welcome the first mailcoach from London. It had left on the Saturday and was due in Edinburgh at 8am. They had to wait a while, but church bells pealing along the Musselburgh road and gunfire from the Castle told everyone that the coach would shortly be rolling up the Canongate. It was twelve hours late which was not at all bad for an inaugural run. Later the *Scotsman* reported that the coach had been arriving earlier and earlier, soon achieving the advertised time and becoming a watchword for punctuality.

This was not the only instance when a mailcoach attracted a large crowd in Edinburgh. All coaches were news carriers, although much of the accuracy was often twisted and embellished on the way. Great events such as Waterloo in 1815 and the passing of the Reform Act in 1832 were quickly spread by coachmen. Earlier, when the previous bill for the Reform Act had failed, a crowd of 5000 awaited the arrival of the London mail. The guard was less than well received when '*not being so communicative as the multitude desired, was rather roughly treated*'.

The single fare for the entire journey to London was £10, much higher than previous stagecoach fares, but it worked out much cheaper than using post-chaises or taking one's own carriage. It compared very well with the five days taken for a stagecoach journey.

Chapter 20

Edinburgh Coach-builders

Coach-building in Edinburgh was thought to have started about 1696 but for some time this was limited to the repair of coaches from London or abroad although a few simple carriages might have been made. It could be said to have started as a proper trade in 1738 when John Home, having finished his apprenticeship with a firm of London coach-builders, returned to Edinburgh with some original ideas of his own. He was particularly interested in using different workmen to make the various parts of a carriage; previously all hands had been expected to be able to make all the constituent parts. He took men on to train and created a band of experts which made for great improvements in coach-building methods.

Soon Edinburgh carriages were being regarded as good as or even better than those produced in London and elsewhere and the Scottish nobility and gentry did not have to be persuaded to buy the local product. Home's fame soon spread and by the 1760s, these now very elegant and fashionable carriages and coaches were being exported to the West Indies and several parts of Europe. One order from Paris was for one thousand carriages to be supplied within three years. It was reported that in 1783 coaches and chaises (a light open carriage) were constructed as elegantly in Edinburgh as anywhere in Europe.

As the 18th century drew to a close, other manufacturers came on the Edinburgh scene; James Macnee & Co. of Fountainbridge, Ramseys of Barnton and Carse & Co. being some of them. Sir John Carr, on his Scottish tour of 1807, saw a display of carriages by a coach-builder called Crichton at his place near Edinburgh; these were one-third cheaper than those in England. How successful these firms were and how long they lasted is not known. There were other centres of coach-building in Scotland: Glasgow, Aberdeen, Perth, Stirling and Greenock but they never appeared to gain the same kudos as their Edinburgh rivals.

The best-known Scottish coach-builder was a late starter compared with the others. John Croall was born in 1791 and started his career in a modest fashion at the age of 19 when he bought a waterlogged barge on the Forth and Clyde Canal, fitted it with wheels and ran his first primitive coach between Stirling and Slamannan, a distance of about 20 miles It appears that at first he drove this himself and later, imbued perhaps with a sense of theatre, he employed a Negro coachman. Within four years he had made enough profit to secure a government contract for the supply of wagons and mail-carts at Portpatrick in Wigtownshire from where, at that time, the ships carrying mails left for Ireland.

When Croall started to make his own coaches, at least one of his competitors (Ramsey of Barnton) was accused of attempting to drive him out of business, but Croall survived this and soon led the field and had it almost to himself. His carriages, mainly at that time for personal use or for post-chaise work, took on allcomers and made their mark throughout the country and abroad – they were fast and light, some no more than 12 cwt. which was half as much as their rivals and apparently much less susceptible to breakdown.

It was natural that John Croall should extend his business to include the running of coach services which were springing up between towns throughout the land. The linking of manufacture and operating was natural enough and conferred many advantages; so many indeed that competitors found it increasingly difficult to continue. He was very astute and sometimes ruthless in his attempts to take over services, using tactics such as running coaches at the same time as rivals but with reduced fares. The inn-keepers who had been operating these services simply could not continue to compete for long and by 1835, every stagecoach from Edinburgh to England through the Borders was run by Croalls and in all probability built by them as well. This indeed was also the case with most of the local services within the Borders. Croalls also controlled the mailcoach operations in Scotland and Ireland.

One of the early stagecoaches built by Croalls of Edinburgh, as depicted in an oil painting of which this is an extract. The route was one between Edinburgh and Dumfries and probably dates from around 1815.

An opportunity came in 1836 for them to become involved with the mailcoaches of the northern division of England for which they had been invited to tender. Whether John decided to have a joint venture with one of his rivals, Robert Wallace of Greenock, is not clear but the contract was awarded to them both to furnish *'efficient carriages for the conveyance of His Majesty's mails for the Northern division of England... .including every expense of drawing them to and from their respective inns, for oiling and greasing them for a period of seven years at 2d per double mile'*. John Vidler had been manufacturing and running the English coaches until that year but had been criticised for the fact that a lack of competition had meant a decline in the standard of mailcoaches. This led to the creation of three districts and the decision to go out to tender.

But all did not go smoothly for the partnership, despite Croall having always stressed the high standard of their coach-building, insisting that not one of his mailcoaches in Scotland, Ireland or northern England had ever suffered a broken axle-tree, something which was all too common with Vidler's coaches. In 1839 for example there were a number of complaints being made that coaches were not being kept in a proper state of repair and were often dirty and shabby. This seems oddly at variance with the reputation Croall had previously enjoyed, but does perhaps indicate the dangers of having to delegate responsibility to persons so far from Edinburgh. But matters got worse, with problems which must have arisen at the manufacturing stage – allegations were made that the vehicles were too heavy for

The peak of coach-building; Croall's mailcoach for the Edinburgh to London service, dating from about 1835.

their intended purpose, being clumsy and defective, particularly as far as their unmatched wheels were concerned. Croalls had either to reduce the weight of their coaches to a standard 18cwt or to withdraw those where this could not be done. Other complaints centred on allegations that properly-seasoned timbers were not being used in the manufacture of the coaches. These problems must have been resolved satisfactorily, for Croalls were again invited to tender in 1843, although this time the rules were more stringent. Again he was awarded the contracts for Scotland, Ireland and Northern England for a period of seven years. This was the last invitation by the Postmaster-General, for the advent of the railways was about to bring the mailcoach to its end.

John spent much of his time travelling, supervising and demonstrating the Croall-built vehicles. When the Tsar of Russia ordered twenty of them, Croall went over and drove the first stagecoach from Moscow to St. Petersburg. Nearer home, James Haig of Bemersyde in the Borders (an ancestor of the Earls Haig) is recorded as having bought a coach from John Croall for £60 in 1826.

John's younger brother Peter worked with him but later the business was divided into two concerns; John leading the operating side from premises in George Street whilst Peter took charge of the coach-building works in York Place. These works were by far the largest of their kind in Scotland, employing about a hundred men at the peak.

To avoid extinction with the demise of coach services from the 1840s onwards, John started a firm of funeral directors which flourished under his name until the middle of this century. He died in 1870 with a life-span which encompassed the glorious years of coaching.

Peter's coach works felt the impact of railways far less, for private carriages would remain in demand until the motorcar arrived early in the 20th century. He had already opened another works in Kelso which were run by his son, also a John. Their carriages were by now quite famous and when they secured a Royal Warrant from Queen Victoria, they had few peers in the field. Coach-building ceased in 1904 and the Edinburgh business was sold in 1928. Known today as Croall Bryson, the business in Kelso flourishes as motor agents with branches at Melrose, Hawick, Duns and Wooler, under Robert Croall, the great-great-grandson of Peter. The original Roxburghshire Works in Bridge Street, Kelso, were demolished in 1996/7 when the firm moved to new premises in the town's industrial estate.

It is fitting that a name long linked with the romance of the coaching industry should be perpetuated in the Borders, through where so many of the Croall coaches had operated.

Chapter 21

Coaches from Edinburgh to London through the Borders

The coach services between the two capitals were the first to be seen in the Borders, for every one of them used a route within the area. None was intended for the use of people in the Borders, other than those taking them from a stopping place to go south. Priority was always given to people making the entire journey and it was only if the coach was not full to start with that people had an opportunity of using these services at intermediate points. It would have been disappointing for someone turning up for such a coach, only to find it full. For this reason, Borderers relied more on their own local services rather than have all the doubts about the more romantic long-distance ones. Mile for mile they were more expensive as well.

In chapter 18, information was given about the early stagecoaches operating between Edinburgh and London prior to 1800. In that year there were three such services, the Royal Mail and the *Royal Union*, both through Berwick and the *Royal Charlotte* through Coldstream. Much later, these were joined by a Night Mail through Kelso, the *Duke of Wellington* (also through Kelso) and the *Chevy Chase* through Jedburgh. These were long considered to be some of the finest of all British services although, as everywhere, they were more to be admired for their fine livery and turn-out than as comfortable means of getting from one place to another.

Services through Berwick

This was the way used by the earliest of the cross-border services. By 1800, the former Newcastle service had been extended to London, leaving Drysdale's Turf Coffee House in South St. Andrews Square. Edinburgh, with overnight stops at Newcastle and York. It was called the *Royal Union* but this was frequently contracted simply to *Union*. It carried four inside passengers at a fare of £7.7s for the total distance, with a reduced cost of £4.4s for those travelling on the outside. Presumably the fare did not include the cost of overnight accommodation at the two intermediate places. During its lifetime, the Edinburgh starting time of 6am never altered, even after change of ownership.

By 1825 it had been scooped up into the Croall empire; it now left from the Black Bull in Catherine Street and the run was made straight through to London without the overnight stops.

With the completion of a rail connection between London, York and Newcastle in 1837, the coach then terminated in Newcastle The service was finally withdrawn with the arrival of the railway in Berwick from Edinburgh in 1846 and at Tweedmouth from Newcastle the following year. Until the Royal Border Bridge was completed in 1850 to join up the two rail systems, passengers were conveyed in an omnibus between both terminals.

Although not a London service, reference is made here to a coach which ran from Edinburgh to Berwick, probably intended to assist people at intermediate points as well as Berwick folk. It was a two-horse light coach called *The Dart*, which started about 1825 and was operated by Croalls from the Black Bull in Edinburgh. The last reference to it was in 1837 so presumably it ceased to run shortly after that. It served Cockburnspath, Reston and Ayton, the only communities of any size on its way through Berwickshire. On its return journey it left the Red Lion and the King's Arms alternately.

As mentioned in chapter 19, the East Coast Royal Mail service between Edinburgh and London commenced in 1786. In Post Office parlance, it was referred to as *The East Road Mail*. In 1800 it left from Drysdale's Turf Coffee House in South St. Andrews Square, every day including Sundays but not Thursdays, taking about 60 hours for the journey. At this time, there were no outside passengers and the fare was £7.7s for the entire distance. By 1806 it was run every day and now carried outside passengers as well at a cost of £4.4s.

The Scottish stages for the mail service were at Haddington and Dunbar in East Lothian and Press in Berwickshire. The journey then went through Berwick and continued to Alnwick, Newcastle, Northallerton, Doncaster, Newark, Baldock, Hatfield, Barnet and London, a total distance of 387 miles. The London terminus was at the Bull and Mouth Inn, off St. Martin's-le-Grand, quite close to the present headquarters of the General Post Office.

From 1824 there were two daily mail services on the East Road. The original one had been taken over by Croalls and now ran from the Black Bull and called at the General Coach Office at 15 Princes Street before leaving Edinburgh. The second ran from The Star Hotel at 36 Princes Street and the White House Coach Office in the evening of alternate days, arriving in 48 hours or, as it was put in the announcement, 'only two nights on the road'. It did not go by Berwick, but took the inland road through Lauder, Gordon, Kelso and Coldstream to Wooler and on to Newcastle to follow the established way southwards to London.

These two mail services endured with only a few minor alterations right through the late 1820s until 1837. In that year, the railway from London had opened northwards as far as Newcastle and, as was the case with the stagecoach, the service from Edinburgh terminated there. It left Edinburgh at 7am, passed through Berwick at 1.46pm (so taking over six hours to get that far) and reached London at 5.28 'on the morning of the second day', an elapsed time of $22^{1}/_{2}$ hours. The night service was withdrawn from the Kelso, Coldstream, Wooler route to Newcastle southwards and now mailbags went to Carlisle.

The mailcoach from London leaving Kelso Square for Edinburgh about 1830.

As with the stagecoach, the end came with the completion of the railway from Edinburgh to Berwick in 1846, marking the end of sixty years of distinguished service. There were now two daily mail services by rail from Edinburgh and the time taken to go to Berwick had been reduced to just under three hours, less than half that taken by the mailcoach at its fastest.

Services through Coldstream

The way via Berwick may have been the first used for cross-border stagecoach travel, but the Coldstream route enjoyed the privilege of being the selected one for the first regular services between the capitals. As mentioned in chapter 18, the original coach had terminated at Newcastle, then was extended to London around 1785 and given the name *Royal Charlotte* (or sometimes *Queen Charlotte*). By 1800 it ran on three days a week, leaving The Black Bull at Catherine Street at the head of Leith Walk. By 1806 the service had become a daily one, other than Sundays.

Shortly after the significant date of 1815, this service underwent important changes, re-emerging as *The Duke of Wellington* to honour the victor of Waterloo. From the beginning it was a superior coach, intended to attract a better kind of custom and it seems to have been very successful. Most ordinary coaches by now were designed to carry eight inside passengers, but this one was restricted to four to allow for greater comfort – which naturally added greatly to the fare. To gain better intermediate connections for passengers, the route no longer went by Greenlaw, but from Lauder via Gordon to Kelso then along the Tweed to Coldstream, over the bridge into Northumberland and on to Newcastle and southwards. Like its predecessor it started at the Black Bull three days a week (Monday, Wednesday and Friday) leaving at 5.30am, calling at Lauder (Black Bull) at 9.30, Gordon at 11.15, Kelso (Cross Keys) at noon and Coldstream at 1pm.

Arriving in London on the third morning, it took approximately 48 hours for the complete journey, the fastest time ever achieved on a regular service. When Croalls took over the service in the 1820s, they regarded it as the flagship of all their routes, and so it remained until 1837 when it terminated at Newcastle to make a railway connection, just as the Mailcoach had done. Like so many other services, by this time the title seems to have been dropped in favour of the more prosaic 'High Flyer', suggesting perhaps that the romanticism of coach travel was fast disappearing. The service had also speeded up, the time to Kelso being reduced from six and a half hours to five. It last ran in 1847 when the rail link between Edinburgh and London was all but in place, other than the short stretch between Berwick and Tweedmouth.

Services through Jedburgh

Although the road between Edinburgh and London via Jedburgh was the shortest distance (365 miles compared with 395 via Berwick and 380 via Coldstream), it took a long time before a service this way ever started. There were a number of reasons for this; principally the poor gradients on the road over the Cheviot Hills at Carter Bar and the lack of facilities between there and Newcastle.

In time these matters were resolved and the first coach service ran in 1830, operated by Croalls from the Black Bull, leaving Edinburgh daily by way of Lauder (Black Bull), St. Boswells, Ancrum, Jedburgh (Spread Eagle) and on by Newcastle southwards to London. Around this time, the road south across the moors from Corbridge to Darlington was made suitable for coach traffic, but this more direct route (now known as the A68) was never used by Scottish stagecoaches, presumably because of the lack of population through the counties of Durham and the North Riding of Yorkshire.

In 1836, with the better roads, it was now possible for London-bound stagecoaches to go through Galashiels for the first time and continue to Jedburgh by way of Melrose. Stops were made at Ford's Inn at Buckholmside ($3^1/_2$ hours from Edinburgh), The George at Melrose (4 hours), and the Spread Eagle at Jedburgh ($5^1/_2$ hours), with the route from there southwards as before. The revised service was given the name of *Chevy Chase*, a reference to the famous ballad of that name which dealt with the feuds of the Border families, Percys and Douglases, in the area of Redesdale through which the coach passed after it entered Northumberland at Carter Bar.

As with the coach services through Berwick and Coldstream, this service terminated at Newcastle in 1837. Just before it was withdrawn in 1847, it took $11^1/_2$ hours to reach Newcastle.

Chapter 22

Stagecoaches from Edinburgh to Border Towns

Prior to 1800, the number of coach services to Border towns from Edinburgh were few and there is little information available on them. Almost coinciding with the start of the new century, a sudden burst of operators clearly reflected the public's desire to travel for the first time on scheduled services. Often rivals ran identical services between towns, occasionally to the same time-table, but with one a little cheaper than the other. The cost of travelling by coach was far beyond the means of ordinary working folk, but professional people readily grasped the opportunity to travel by this convenient if not comfortable method. Stagecoaches were to be the backbone of a public transport service until finally killed off when the railways arrived in the Borders from the mid-1840s onwards, but in their half century of use, they had completely transformed the concept of travel.

The railway companies emphasised their debt to coach operators in a number of ways: the word *coach* itself has been perpetuated to this day to signify a passenger-carrying railway wagon and the early such wagons were even painted to resemble the livery of a stagecoach. The guard's title was similarly retained from the coaching age, even if he were no longer issued with weapons at the start of the journey. In some of the early trains, the guard was even perched precariously on top of one of the carriages, just as they had done on mailcoaches.

Kelso Services

The first regular coach ran about 1795 from the White Swan Inn at Kelso to McFarlanes at the head of Canongate in Edinburgh on Mondays and Wednesdays, taking about 10 hours. The return journeys were on Tuesdays and Thursdays. The fare was 14 shillings. It was commonly referred to as the 'Kelso Fly' and was mentioned in this way by Walter Scott when he used it to convey manuscripts to his publisher John Ballantyne in Edinburgh. The route taken was by Lauder and Smailholm, with changes of horses at these places in the Borders.

In 1804, a competitor appeared, announcing in the Kelso Mail on 5th March that the Kelso coach for Edinburgh would set out from the Cross Keys every Monday and Wednesday, reaching Edinburgh in time for dinner, returning from the White

Horse, Canongate every Tuesday and Thursday. Tickets for the whole road were lowered to 7 shillings, but half that for passengers travelling outside. Three days later another announcement was made by the original operator that the *old* coach continues to run from the White Swan every Monday and Wednesday, returning on Tuesdays and Thursdays, at fares of 10s6d for inside passengers and 6s.for those on the outside. Although reduced, these new prices were still more than that charged by their competitor. The extraordinary thing about these competitors is that they left Kelso and Edinburgh at the same time on the same days of the week and though there is no record of it, speeding and other forms of dangerous driving were probably quite common as they vied with one another to be first at the destination.

Map 27 – Kelso Town Centre 1823, showing the Coaching Inns: 1 Cross Keys, 2 White Swan, 3 Queen's Head, 4 Red Lion. (from John Wood's Map)

By 1806, things had settled down a little in that they each charged the same reduced fare of 10s6d. (6s outside). The Cross Keys coach now added Saturday to their running days and, not to be outdone, the White Swan did the same.

This state of rivalry continued for a number of years, the one change being that an additional stop was made at Earlston in each direction, necessitating a detour from the direct route.

By 1820 both had acquired names. The one to the Cross Keys in Kelso now ran from McGregors at 117 High Street, Edinburgh on the same three days as before, but now extended its journey through to Coldstream. The earliest records show the name of the coach as *The Commercial Traveller* but soon this was contracted to *The Traveller* even in official notices. These were the active days in the lifetime of coach services and the Edinburgh inns acting as departure and arrival points seemed to change quite frequently. The other service to The White Swan in Kelso now left Waldie's at 1 North Bridge, adorned with the name *Tweedside*.

Early in the 1830s, the *Traveller* ceased running, leaving the *Tweedside* as the sole local coach to Kelso from Edinburgh. It was now a daily service, leaving the capital at 8am, arriving at Lauder at 12.30, Earlston at 1.30 and the Kelso White Swan at 2pm. About 1840 the daily service was doubled by an afternoon service in each direction and now the journey time had been reduced from six hours to five and a half.

The Edinburgh to Kelso local service was one of the few which had not been taken over by Croalls in the early competitive decades of the century, but they finally did so in 1848, possibly at a time when the Kelso operator was beginning to realise that the coming of the railways would put an end to the enterprise. Whether Croalls were more optimistic is a matter for conjecture, but they introduced a fast five hour service for the first time, still using the name of *Tweedside*.

The following year the railway arrived at Newtown (later to become Newtown St. Boswells) and a local service called Abbotsford Coaches ran from the Cross Keys in Kelso to the station there via Mertoun Bridge and St. Boswells, leaving at 9am in time for the 10.45 to Edinburgh. Then at 2.45pm another coach ran via Rutherford, Maxton and St. Boswells in time for the 4.30 train. An advertisement in the Kelso Mail on 1st March 1849 announced that Kelso people would have at least four hours in Edinburgh if they use these facilities. This could never have been achieved with any direct coach and it is rather surprising that Croalls persisted with their service.

Even after the railway arrived at Kelso on 17th June 1850, the stagecoach to Edinburgh continued, although the service had been reduced to three times weekly in each direction; indicating that Croalls were now using only one coach. This was in fact the last coach service to the central Borders and when it was finally withdrawn in 1852, the only remaining service from Edinburgh was the one to Peebles. As the railways were carrying Borderers to the capital in half the time and at half the cost, the demise of the coaches had been certain when the first train whistle sounded.

Kelso's original station was at Wallacenick, just over a mile from the town centre, but in January 1851 the line was extended to the site at Maxwellheugh across the Tweed from the town where it was to remain during the lifetime of the railway system.

Although not far from the centre, a steep hill had to be negotiated after crossing the Tweed bridge and it soon became necessary to provide a form of transport for passengers from the station to the Cross Keys and return. A vehicle known as an omnibus designed to carry up to thirty passengers was used for this and like elsewhere it proved very popular for short journeys. This load of passengers could have been tackled quite easily by one horse on level ground, but because of the hill to Maxwellheugh, the Kelso station omnibus used a pair. This service endured until the introduction of motorised transport in the early part of the 20th century.

Jedburgh Services

The starting date of this service is not known, but was probably just a year or two before it was first recorded in the Edinburgh Post Office Directory in 1800. Like the Kelso one, it was known as 'The Fly' and was described by one writer as *'The wretched Jedburgh Fly'*. In those years, it left Edinburgh on Wednesdays and Saturdays and went by way of Lauder and Drygrange (Flybridge), with changes of horses at The Black Bull and Salmon respectively. At Jedburgh, it terminated at an inn also called The Black Bull. This was in the Castlegate and appeared to have been in use for coaching before the popular Spread Eagle in the High Street took its place. The fare was advertised as 14s for the journey. Later the days were changed to Mondays and Thursdays.

Around 1818, a new service to replace the former one began on an entirely new route to Jedburgh. In that year, as referred to in chapter 11, a new road was constructed on the left bank of the Gala Water through Stow, so enabling an easier journey to Jedburgh, with the added advantage of serving the expanding industrial town of Galashiels as well as Melrose. Up to this time, neither of these places had enjoyed a stagecoach facility through them.

This new service was dreamt up by Walter Caverhill, the then innkeeper at the Spread Eagle in the Jedburgh High Street, who saw it as an opportunity to enhance his business. It was a four-horse coach which left the Star Hotel in Princes Street three days a week, returning from Jedburgh on the alternate days, the cost being 16s. for inside and 12s outside. To celebrate the victory at Waterloo a few years before, it was decided to name the coach *Prince Blücher* after the Prussian General who played such a decisively important part in the battle. Soon the name was shortened to *The Blücher*.

On this new route, horses were changed at the newly-built Torsonce Inn at Stow, then either at Ford's at Buckholmside (for Galashiels) or the George at Melrose.

Around 1825, another name also appeared, the *Royal Express*. It seems that this and *The Blücher* referred to the same Edinburgh to Jedburgh service, running between the same inns. Perhaps of the three weekly coaches, one of then carried the new name, or as has been suggested, one name was used from Edinburgh and the other for the return journey. Often the titles seem to be used indiscriminately which only compounds the mystery. It was the only instance in the Borders of two titles for a coach service being used at the same time.

This service had an untroubled time until 1837, when Croalls started a daily service to Jedburgh from their offices at 2 Princes Street This competition seems to have been too much and by 1840, Croalls had the field to themselves, although the service was no longer a daily one. It reverted to three days a week, just as the former coach had done before Croalls came upon the scene, taking about six and a half hours to complete the journey.

By 1847, the service was still three times weekly but had been speeded up, almost as if to compete with the railway soon to come to Galashiels and Melrose. In what appears to have been a joint operation with Scotts, it now took four hours to reach Melrose and five and a half to Jedburgh, making it an hour quicker than before. The return journey was even faster, taking only five hours for the complete journey.

With the arrival of the railway line from Edinburgh to Hawick in November 1849, the Jedburgh coach was terminated, being replaced by two local services from Jedburgh to the nearest railway stations. The first was a four-times daily omnibus from the Spread Eagle to New Belses Station a few miles to the west of Ancrum. The other was a twice-daily from the Harrow Inn, Jedburgh, to Newtown. These services continued to connect Jedburgh with the outside world until their own railway line arrived in 1856, this event marking the end of public coach travel in the town.

Selkirk, Hawick, Carlisle and North-west England Services

This route took a long time to establish itself, mainly because of the lack of demand for coach travel by local people early in the 19th century but also the poor state of the turnpike road which ran down the right bank of the Gala Water through Stagehall. One lonely coach made its way three times weekly to Carlisle in 1800, leaving the Black Bull in Catherine Street at the head of Leith Walk in Edinburgh. Horses were changed either at The Queen's Head at Bankhouse or at Stagehall, then the Cross Keys at Selkirk and at the Tower Inn at Hawick. Services also called at the Mosspaul Inn on the Dumfriesshire border, but at that time there were no horse-changing facilities there. Subsequent stops were made at the George at Langholm, the Graham's Arms at Longtown, finishing at the Bush Coffee House in Carlisle. The fare for the entire journey was £1.17s.

In 1806 the service was given the title of *Star Coach* and extended southwards to Liverpool and Manchester.

The first mailcoach on the same route ran on 14th August 1807, replacing the horse-post which had sufficed until then. Known as the *West Mail*, it also left from the Black Bull, Edinburgh daily (excluding Thursday but including Sunday). It used the same stages as the other service and for over ten years the two were the only forms of public transport available in the valley of the Gala Water and through Selkirk and Hawick.

In 1819 the new road on the left bank of the Gala Water was completed and the bridge over the river at Bowland (built in 1815) now created a connection with the older road at Crosslee and on via Clovenfords and the Yair Bridge to Selkirk. With the improved road, it was possible to provide a quicker service, especially for the mailcoach. The published times for this were; from Edinburgh Black Bull at 7am, Selkirk 11.27, Hawick 12.51pm, Mosspaul 2.31, Langholm 3.57 and Carlisle 5.50pm. As with the stagecoach, this mail service was also extended to Liverpool and Manchester. North of Selkirk, the changing of the horses was now done at the Torsonce Inn at Stow in Midlothian and, further north, at Fushiebridge in the same county.

In 1822, the old stagecoach was replaced with a new light coach, still running on three days of the week, but now rejoicing in the name of *Sir Walter Scott*, marking perhaps the creation of his baronetcy in that year. At least in the earlier years, Walter Scott himself had often used the mailcoach as far as the Yair bridge, where his own carriage would be waiting to take him to his home at Ashiestiel, a few miles distant up the south bank of the Tweed, It is not known whether he ever travelled in his namesake.

The residents of Hawick had been complaining about the high cost of seats to Edinburgh on these two coaches (inside 28s, outside 20s) and in 1822, following a chance meeting with 'a Mr. Croall from Edinburgh', help was given to inaugurate a competitive coach from Hawick to Edinburgh which commenced the following year and continued to run until the railway arrived in Hawick in 1849. This coach was called the *Standard*.

In 1832, the final major change was made on this route, the creation of the new road between Galashiels and Selkirk. This meant that for the first time scheduled coaches ran through Galashiels, where calls were made at the Bridge Inn to pick up and drop passengers.

About this time, all references to the *Sir Walter Scott* had gone and it appears that Croalls had acquired both services, discontinuing one and running the *Standard* to Carlisle and on to Liverpool and Manchester.

Carlisle was connected by rail to the south in 1846 and the first effects of this were being felt north of the border as well. By then there had been two mailcoaches on this route, the *Day Mail* and *Night Mail*, but now these were both terminated at Carlisle. The mails from these coaches were transferred to the railway at Carlisle Station and from there went to Euston Grove Station in London. In the same year the stagecoach to Liverpool and Manchester terminated at Preston where people could continue by train southwards. Three years later, the Night Mail to Carlisle was withdrawn.

By 1847, the fastest times were being achieved to Carlisle, both by the mail and the stagecoach:

	Miles	**Departure Time**	**Elapsed Time**
Mailcoach			
Edinburgh	–	5.38am	–
Torsonce	25	8.07	2hr 29min
Selkirk	39	9.34	3hr 56min
Hawick	51	10.51	5hr 13min
Langholm	73	1.18pm	7hr 40min
Carlisle	94	3.18pm(arrival)	9hr 40min
Stagecoach (Croalls)			
Edinburgh	–	12.45pm	–
Hawick	51	6.00pm	5hr 15min
Carlisle	94	11.30pm(arrival)	10hr 45min

The return journeys took 9 hours 53 minutes and 10 hours respectively. Why the southbound journey on the stagecoach should have taken over an hour more to reach Carlisle is not known, unless there was an error in the Edinburgh Post Office Directory for that year.

The different way of showing the times shows very clearly the way in which the Post Office was obsessed by time-keeping, working to the minute in the published timetables rather than the less onerous quarter hours used by the stagecoach operators.

In 1849, the Post Office decided that the Edinburgh mails for Carlisle should now be sent by road to Carstairs in Lanarkshire to connect with the recently constructed railway between Carlisle and Glasgow. This brought an end to the mailcoach on the Edinburgh-Hawick-Carlisle run. In the same year the new railway from Edinburgh was completed as far as Hawick, although it would be another thirteen years before the final link through to Carlisle was completed. Croalls cancelled the Edinburgh to Carlisle coach, replacing it with a daily service to and from Hawick. Unsurprisingly, this did not last very long and was soon dropped.

A new service was inaugurated to connect Hawick with Carlisle, leaving the Tower Inn daily. Almost as if anticipating what its fate would be when the final stretch of railway was completed, the coach was given the eerily portentous title of *Engineer*.

Selkirk was now the only town on this route without a direct railway connection and until this finally arrived from Galashiels in 1856, an omnibus ran twice daily between the County Hotel in Selkirk and the station at Galashiels.

On the first of July 1862, the last section of the Edinburgh to Carlisle railway was completed from Hawick southwards. The North British Railway Company gave the new link to the border the name *Waverley Line*, one which was to become famous in the annals of railway history. The last coach used between Hawick and Carlisle, the *Engineer*, was taken off, apparently travelling in ignominy on the first train southwards from Hawick.

Duns Services

This was one of the few straightforward routes in the Borders. The service appears to have left from the premises at 1 North Bridge during its entire lifetime and taken the same route on existing roads through Lauder and Greenlaw, with changes of horses at the Black Bull and the Crown Inn respectively. It started as a daily service about 1820, was named *Royal Eagle* and was a light coach drawn by two horses. The Duns terminus was at the Black Bull in the street of the same name.

It ceased running in 1849 when the branch line from the main line at Reston to Duns was completed. From then on, an omnibus ran from The White Swan in Duns Market Place to the railway station, a distance of about a mile.

In his book on Greenlaw, 'An Old Berwickshire Town', Robert Gibson wrote in 1905 about a two-horse coach the *Eclipse* which ran through that town about 1840. Could this have been the Duns coach hiding under a different name?

Peebles Services

The first reference to this route appeared in 1795 but it probably started just a few years before then. It was operated by William Wilson with his 'caravan' – a two-wheeled vehicle drawn by one horse, probably little more than a small cart with some form of awning over it. It left from Fortune's in Chapel Street, Edinburgh on Tuesdays and Fridays, arriving at Peebles ten hours later. The return journeys were on the following days. Little is known about the journey itself apart from reference to a stop at Howgate in Midlothian for a *'drap of kail'* at Tibby's (and probably a drap of something else as well). The fare for the journey was at first 6s but by 1800 had increased to 7s.

The caravan was replaced by a light two-horse coach in 1806 which ran in half the time of its predecessor. Known as the *'Peebles Fly'*, it ran from Mackay's in the Grassmarket, Edinburgh, on Tuesdays, Thursdays and Saturdays, returning from Peebles on the same day. The way now went by Penicuik where the horses would have been changed. In their *History of Peebles*, Brown and Lawson recorded that this coach was an old post-chaise, painted green and picked out with red, with three yellow wheels and one black one. Unusually it appeared to carry mailbags, the only recorded instance of this method of transport being used in the Borders by the Post Office. For journeys such as this, they usually used mailcarts or postboys on horseback.

In 1825 the service was taken over by Waldie's from their premises at 1 North Bridge, Edinburgh, taking three hours to the Harrow Hotel (now the County Hotel) in Peebles carrying six passengers at a reduced fare of 5s. Within a short time, McGregor's at 177 High Street, Edinburgh, joined in with a competing coach

Both services had changed hands by 1831, now being operated by Browns and Crolls. They left Edinburgh daily at the same time, but Brown's coach was extended through to Innerleithen, so giving that town its first such service. Some years later, Crolls had successfully squeezed out the opposition to became the sole operator for the route with the one daily service in either direction, but they did continue with the Innerleithen service.

In 1852, Croall's were no longer taking this coach service to Innerleithen, but they substituted a separate local one from the Tontine Hotel, Peebles to the St. Ronan's Inn, Innerleithen, twice daily (but only once on Wednesdays).

The North British Railway completed their line to Peebles from Edinburgh on 18th August 1855 and Croall's withdrew their coach on the same day. The Innerleithen coach survived however and lasted until the railway was extended eastwards from Peebles to Galashiels in 1866.

West Linton Services

West Linton (or simply Linton as it was once known) in the far north-west of the Borders area is on the main road from Edinburgh to Biggar. This was the route used by many of the long-distance stagecoaches from the capital to Dumfries (The *Royal George* and later the *Robert Burns* for example) but as these coaches did not serve the Borders, they are beyond the scope of this book. But West Linton did have a local coach service to and from Edinburgh which first appears in records at the late date of 1847. It left Alexander's in West Linton daily, taking two hours to reach Taylor's in Edinburgh. As elsewhere, the service ceased with the arrival of the railway in 1864.

Moffat and Dumfries Services

Peeblesshire with its small and scattered population meant that coach services in the county were sparse. One route which was reasonable well used by carriages was that to Moffat by way of Broughton and Tweedsmuir. But these were not stagecoaches; for various attempts to run such a service on this route had been tried, but had all failed due to the lack of passengers along the way, the alternative way via Biggar being preferred. There never was a regular service other than the mailcoach, although, as mentioned in chapter 12, there must have been a sufficient number of private carriages using the route to justify three coaching inns in Tweedsmuir.

The mailcoach started running to Dumfries on 5th May 1806, from Drysdale's, Turf Coffee House, at No.1 South St. Andrews Square, Edinburgh. It ran three days a week and carried passengers with fares at 18s for inside travel and 12s outside. It replaced a horse-post which could no longer cope with the large amount of mail destined for Ireland by way of the Irish Mail through Dumfries to Stranraer. Most of the mail from England went this way to Ireland, this being the shortest and most reliable sea crossing before the introduction of steamships.

By 1825 the mail service was taken over by Crualls, now running daily from the Black Bull Inn in Catherine Street as well as the General Coach Office at 15 Princes Street.

The route until 1833 went through West Linton (where horses were changed) then followed a poor road southwards to Blyth Bridge. In that year the route was altered to give a more direct one from Edinburgh through Leadburn and Noblehouse (horse-change) to meet the former road at Blyth Bridge. From there the way southwards was common to both, proceeding through Broughton, Rachan Mill and on to the Crook Inn in Tweedsmuir for another change of horses before the long climb into Dumfriesshire and on to Moffat.

Various departure times were tried from Edinburgh, mostly in the morning but there were a few in the evening as well in the 1830s.

This mailcoach finished even earlier than the one to Carlisle, for by 1847 the mail for Dumfries and Ireland from Edinburgh was going to Carstairs to be taken further by rail. With the withdrawal of the mail service, the post office once more reverted to horseposts and mailcarts to get the letters to the remote Tweedsmuir settlements.

Chapter 23

Stagecoaches on Cross Routes

During the entire era of stagecoaches in the Borders, apart from those to and from Edinburgh, there were only a few services to provide cross-routes. All but one started from Kelso, so substantiating the claim made that the town had been the hub of the coach system in the Borders.

Kelso to Berwick-upon-Tweed

This cross-service started about 1825, running three times a week in each direction via Coldstream. By 1830 it acquired the name of *The Tweedside Coach* which must have confused everyone as a coach of the same name also went at that period from the same inn at Kelso to Edinburgh. That inn was the White Swan and the coach left here at 8am daily, arriving at the Hen and Chickens Inn and the Nag's Head Inn in Berwick on alternate days. It left Berwick at 3pm, other than on Saturdays when it was later at 5pm. On Fridays, an additional coach left Berwick at 8.30am, starting the return journey from Kelso at 4.30pm.

As bookings for this coach could also be made at Hownam's Commercial Inn at Coldstream, this was probably where a stop was made. As far as is known, there were no staging facilities at Coldstream, so the horses may have been changed at the Collingwood Arms in Cornhill just across the Tweed. These services appeared to be for the summer – those for the winter period would have been less than daily.

In 1833, the Hen and Chickens Inn in Berwick was the only terminus for the *Tweedside*, although the times were unchanged. Competition arrived in the same year in the form of the *Border Union* which ran 'in the bathing season' every morning from the King's Arms in Berwick to the Cross Keys in Kelso, returning the same day. Reference to the bathing season is somewhat puzzling, for the coach left Berwick in the morning and not the other way around. This meant that the owners could not have been referring to passengers using the coach to have a dip in the sea, but rather to mean 'during the summer months'.

With the arrival of the railway at Kelso in 1850, the former services disappeared, to be replaced with one which ran from Jedburgh (Spread Eagle Inn) to Berwick through Kelso on Mondays, Wednesdays and Fridays. The return journey was on Tuesday, Thursday and Saturday. This was also withdrawn six years later when the railway finally arrived at Jedburgh.

Hawick to Kelso

This service started as a twice weekly one about 1822, calling at Jedburgh. Known as the *Favorite*, it left Hawick at 8am, Jedburgh at 10 and arrived at the Cross Keys in Kelso at noon. The return journey left Kelso at 4pm, Jedburgh 6pm, reaching Hawick at 8pm.

In the summer months, some services were run between Hawick and Berwick through Kelso, but references to them were sporadic at best and it is not known how regularly they ran.

The *Favorite* was withdrawn in 1850, leaving only a rump service east of Jedburgh as mentioned in the Kelso to Berwick section above.

Kelso to Glasgow

This long route started operations in June 1835 and was the first and only one to link the central Border towns. Its full title was the *Tweed and Clydesdale Union Coach* which left the Cross Keys in Kelso at 6am daily, calling at Melrose, Galashiels, Innerleithen, Peebles, Biggar and Lanark, reaching Glasgow at 7pm. The return journey left the Mail Office at 64 Trongate, Glasgow, at the same time of 6am and reaching Kelso at 7pm. The comments in the announcement in the Kelso Mail of 10th June are worth repeating:

> *'It is perhaps unnecessary to enumerate the many objects of beauty and interest which are to be found on the line of road through which this Coach passes - it holds out inducement to the lover of the picturesque, the inquirer after health and the man of business. The Proprietors, having done everything in their power to render this conveyance worthy of public patronage, would fain hope that it will meet with that support of which it is deserving.'*

Unfortunately few details of this service have ever been recorded; several mentions are made in passing about the coach at the towns through which it went, but how well used it was and when it was withdrawn are not known.

Selkirk to Moffat

On the wall of the County Hotel in Selkirk there hangs an old advertisement for a coach called *The Flower of Yarrow* which ran from Selkirk to St. Mary's Loch to connect there with the *Ettrick Shepherd* coach to Moffat. The service commenced on 31st May 1887 and ran on the mornings of Tuesdays, Thursdays and Saturdays until the end of September, returning in time for the evening trains. It does appear to have been little more than an early omnibus with rows of seats on top facing each side as well as in the middle. It has been suggested that it may have done a circular journey to include the Ettrick valley to deliver supplies as well as taking passengers. Apart from minor services from towns to the nearest railway station, this was probably the last scheduled coach in the Borders. It is not known when it ceased to operate.

Presumably the *Ettrick Shepherd* was a similar kind of vehicle running between Moffat and St. Mary's Loch.

Chapter 24

Postscript

John Croall of Edinburgh (born 1791, died 1870), was perhaps the chief protagonist of the Scottish stagecoaching tradition. During his life he witnessed and indeed helped to create the most important aspects of this dramatic form of transport. By the time he died, long-distance coaches had been withdrawn from all but the most isolated parts of Scotland.

As earlier chapters have shown, the coming of the railways brought about the demise of the stagecoach, bringing for the first time cheap travel in modest comfort within the reach of virtually everyone. As most of the goods on the carriers' wagons were also transferred to the railway companies, the number of road users quickly diminished from the 1850s onwards and on the country roads of the Borders the only vehicles left were private carriages and farm carts.

Not surprisingly, toll revenue dropped sharply and it soon became evident that there would be insufficient funds to keep the highways in good condition. The burden had to be transferred to the property-owners, giving rise to what is now generally known as the rating system based on property values. This led to the disbanding of turnpike trusts and any powers remaining with them soon becoming assimilated with the growing county councils. The roads were no longer considered very important and by the end of the century many of them were in a poor state of repair.

It took a turn of events of another kind in the early days of this century to change everything – the invention of the internal combustion engine suddenly made any other forms of road transport look archaic. The motor-car, motor-bus and lorry were now the masters of the highway and inevitably this led to a reversal of the railways' fortune. The roads became important again and it was not long before most of the main ones in the Borders had a sealed surface, by courtesy of the earlier genius of McAdam coupled with the advances made with tar and asphalt.

In the 1920s and 1930s, the flexibility of bus services began to be the downfall of railway branch lines. Similarly, lorries could take goods from the factory to the shop and warehouse without having to load and off-load at railway terminals. These factors led to the first rail closures, those of the service from Fountainhall to Lauder in 1932 and that from Leadburn through West Linton to Dolphinton the following year. Flooding in August 1948 seriously damaged the railway line between Duns and St. Boswells and that from Roxburgh to Jedburgh – neither was ever reopened. The line to Selkirk went in 1951 together with Reston to Duns in the same year. From 1962 onwards the closures became contagious; Riccarton Junction to Hexham, Peebles to Galashiels, St. Boswells to Kelso and Berwick, Symington to Peebles and Edinburgh to Peebles. Finally in the central Borders the Waverley route from Edinburgh to Carlisle through Galashiels and Hawick was closed on 6th January 1969.

The only railway line remaining in the Borders was the main one from Edinburgh (Waverley) to London (King's Cross) but with a shrug of indignity they left no station open within the region. The nearest now are at Dunbar and Berwick in the east and at Carlisle in the south-west.

Once again the highways rule, just as they did in the early decades of the 19th century. What would Thomas Telford and John Croall have made of that?

Appendix A

Bibliography

Much of the material for this book has been obtained from the books and other publications referred to below. Many of these are long out of print but most are available from the Scottish Borders Library service, either from their own stocks or by special arrangement with other libraries throughout the country.

The Borders:

The Scottish Border and Northumberland, John Talbot White, Eyre Methuen, London, 1973.

The Scottish Borderland - The Place and the People, The Border Country Life Association, edited by Richard Allan and Isobel Canlish 1988.

The Borders Book, edited by Donald Omand, Birlinn Ltd., Edinburgh, 1995.

Borders and Berwick, C.A.Strang, The Rutland Press 1994.

Rutherford's Southern Counties Register, (Roxburgh, Berwick and Selkirk) 1866 - reprinted by Border Regional Council 1990.

The Scottish Borders (with Galloway) to 1603 - W.R. Kermack - Johnston & Bacon, 1967.

Highways and Byways in the Border, Andrew and John Lang, Macmillan & Co., 1914.

Counties:

The Royal Commission on the Ancient Monuments of Scotland, HMSO, Edinburgh:-

> *Berwickshire*, 1915.
> *Peeblesshire*, 1967.
> *Roxburghshire*, 1956.
> *Selkirkshire*, 1957.

History of Peeblesshire by T.W.Buchan 1925.

Counties of Peebles and Selkirk by Geo.C.Pringle, 1914.

The History and Antiquities of Roxburghshire and Adjacent Districts by Alexander Jeffrey. First Edition 1836, revised edition 1864.

A History of the Border Counties (Roxburgh, Selkirk, Peebles) by Sir George Douglas, William Blackwood & Sons, 1899.

The History of Berwickshire's Towns and Villages by Elizabeth Laythe, Entire Productions, 1994.

Specific Towns or districts:

The Stow of Wedale by Thomas Wilson (Minister of Stow) - Aberdeen Newspapers Ltd., 1924

The Life and Times of Berwick-upon-Tweed by Raymond Lamont-Brown, John Donald Publishers, Edinburgh, 1988.

Melrose 1826, Melrose Historical Association, edited by D.M.Hood, no date.

History of Peebles 1850-1890 by Brown & Lawson 1950.

Tweedsmuir by Sheila Scott, Biggar, 1995.

Account of the Town of Kelso by John Haig, Edinburgh, 1825.

Guid Auld Galashiels by Margaret C. Lawson, 1997.

Change at St. Boswells - F.G.Peake (Peake Pasha) - Pub. privately 1961.

Roads and Transport:

The Great North Road - The Old Mail Road to Scotland (York to Edinburgh) by Charles G. Harper 1901.

The Great North Road by Norman W. Webster - Bath, Adams and Dart 1974.

The British Mailcoach, Bulletin of the GB Postal History Group of the Postal History Society.

'Postmaster's General Reports', Post Office Archives, London.

The Roads that went to Edinburgh - Proceedings of The Society of Antiquaries of Scotland, Vol L 1915-16 Harry R.G. Inglis.

Roads and Loads in Scotland and Beyond edited by Alexander Fenton and Geoffrey Stell, John Donald Publishers Ltd, Edinburgh, 1984.

Life of Thomas Telford, Civil Engineer, 'written by himself', edited by John Rickman, 1838.

Journal of a Tour of Scotland 1819 by R. Southey.

The History of Coaches by G. A. Thrupp, London 1877.

John Loudon McAdam by Roy Devereux, London, 1930.

The Drove Roads of Scotland by A.R.B. Haldane, David and Charles, 1973.

Coaching Days in Scotland by Victor de Spiganovicz, The Border Magazine Volume XXXI.

Transactions of Hawick Archaeological Society:
Locomotion in Former Days, Walter Wilson, 1874.
Reminiscences of Old Coaching Days, William Murray, 1904.

To Move with the Times - The Story of Transport and Travel in Scotland by Anne Gordon, Aberdeen University Press, 1988.

Stage-Coach to John O'Groats by Leslie Gardiner, Hollis & Carter, 1961.

The Coaching Life by Harry Hanson, Manchester University Press, 1983.

The Roads of Mediaeval Lauderdale, by R.P.Hardie - Oliver & Boyd, Edinburgh, 1942.

Miscellaneous:

Parliamentary Papers, Misc. Volume 5, 1808-1889.

The Social Life of Scotland in the Eighteenth Century by Henry Grey Graham, pub. Adam and Charles Black, London, 1906.

Scotland 1689 to the Present by William Ferguson (The Edinburgh History of Scotland), Volume 4, Oliver and Boyd, 1968.

Scotland's Roman Remains - Lawrence Keppie - John Donald Publishers, Edinburgh, 1986.

First Statistical Account - 1793/1799.

New Statistical Account - 1830 [known as the Second]

Slater's Commercial Directory of Scotland, 1852.

Pigot & Co's Directory 1835-6 and 1837.

Casey's Itinerary 1810.

The Scotch Itinerary, 2nd edition, James Duncan, Glasgow, 1808.

Sir Walter's Post-Bag. Written and selected by Wilfrid Partington, John Murray, London, 1932.

James Dickson and His Legacy by Audrey Mitchell, Kelso, 1997.

The Steel Bonnets by George MacDonald Fraser, Collins Harvill, 1971 reprinted 1986

Post Office Directories of Edinburgh from 1795 onwards (Edinburgh Public Library).

Local Newspapers, especially the Kelso Mail which gives a wealth of information on most parts of the Borders - seen at Archives at Library Headquarters, Selkirk.

Minutes of Turnpike Trustees (various) - seen at Archives at Library Headquarters, Selkirk.

Unpublished manuscripts relating to coaches in Scotland, in the archives of Royal Museum of Scotland, Edinburgh.

Appendix B

Maps

This book would not have been possible without reference to maps of every description and poring over these fascinating documents is for me one of the chief pleasures in the work of research.

I have already acknowledged the help given by the Map Library of the National Library of Scotland. They hold most if not all of the maps noted below (but not necessarily the originals of the rarer ones) and arrangements can usually be made with them at 33 Salisbury Place, Edinburgh EH9 1SL for copies to be ordered. These are very reasonably priced and a valuable tool for anyone embarking on this type of work.

County Maps:

A Map of Roxburghshire or Tiviotdale by Matthew Stobie, 1770 (one inch to the mile).

A Map of the County of Berwick by Captain Armstrong and Son, 1771 (one inch to the mile) Although these two maps were produced within one year of one another, it appears that the actual surveys must have been made some time apart, as some roads which leave one county do not yet appear in the other.

A Map of Selkirkshire or Ettrick Forest by John Ainslie, 1772 (one inch to the mile).

Selkirkshire by John Thomson & Co., 1824. (about one and a fifth miles to the inch). This handsome and beautifully engraved map gives a wealth of detail and a comparison with the county as surveyed by Ainslie in 1772 tells much about the developments which took place in these fifty years.

A New and Correct Map of the Shire of Peebles or Tweeddale by William Edgar 1742. (about one and a seventh miles to the inch).One of the earliest of the Border county maps which well illustrates just how empty Peeblesshire was then.

A Map of the County of Peebles or Tweeddale by M. J. Armstrong 1775 (one inch to the mile), includes a plan of the Town of Peebles.

Town Plans:

These have appeared in various formats for Border towns, the best known being the series produced by **John Wood** from 1818 onwards and collected in 1828 in **The Town Atlas of Scotland.** These maps are accurate and well-engraved, giving a wealth of detail including the names of occupiers of individual buildings. In the Borders, they were made for Hawick, Jedburgh, Melrose, Kelso, Selkirk and Peebles.

Two others I have found of much interest are the **Town Plan of Jedburgh** by **John Ainslie** c1775 which carries charming notes on the state of the roads into the town. **The Plan of the Lands and Barony of Galashiels** by **W. Fairbairn** (1795) is more of a parish than a town map, but it shows only too well just how small the town was in that year. People interested in field names will find it a gem.

Early Road Maps:

A Pocket Guide to the English Traveller, being a compleat Survey and Admeasurement of all the Principal Roads and most considerable Cross-Roads in England and Wales (Thomas Gardner, London 1719) contains the road from Carlisle to Berwick which passes through the Border towns of Castleton, Jedborough(sic) and Kelso. This is probably the earliest map to show any road in detail through the Borders area.

The Survey and Maps of the Roads of North Britain or Scotland (Taylor & Skinner, 1776) were the first detailed road maps, produced in strip form and covering most of the important turnpike roads at that time.

An Actual Survey of the Great Post Roads between London and Edinburgh (M. J. Armstrong, 1776) Produced in the same year as the Taylor & Skinner series, but instead of strip maps, these show the areas surrounding the highway and so give a lot more information on connecting roads. Opposite each map is a list of the local land-owners, post-road distances and inns.

Ordnance Survey Maps:

These maps represented a great forward stride for cartography in that the entire country was accurately surveyed for the first time in a systematic way. They were published from the late 1840s onwards, the ones most used in the preparation of this book being the one inch to a mile (1:63360) and the highly detailed six inch series (1:10560). In the latter every building is marked and there is sufficient detail to satisfy the most demanding historian.

The one inch to the mile series is the one which has been most regularly updated and since the early 1970s has been changed by introducing a metric scale of 1:50000 or about one and a quarter inches to the mile to give increased clarity to the detail. These are available at most book-shops in the Ordnance Survey *Landranger* series and there is also the companion *Pathfinder* maps at the enhanced scale of 1:25000 or about $2^1/2$ inches to the mile.

A word of warning - there are a number of companies which specialise in providing reprints of the early Ordnance Survey maps and these are extensively advertised to give the impression that what is produced is a facsimile of the first editions from the middle of the last century. What is often supplied however are copies of editions dating from about the 1890s – and these can show a very different picture, especially in the growing urban areas. The Map Library in Edinburgh will supply you with the edition you require.

General:

The **Military Survey of Scotland** carried out by **General William Roy** between 1747 and 1755 covers mainland Scotland on a scale of one inch to the mile. Although carried out primarily to assist the authorities had there been a further Jacobite uprising, today it is very useful as it gives an excellent and reasonably accurate picture of what the countryside looked like at that time. The original manuscripts are in the British Library in London, but the Map Library in Edinburgh holds photocopies which may be inspected. For simplicity, throughout this book, these maps are indicated simply as Roy 1750.

Southern Scotland by J. and J. Ainslie, 1789. An interesting map, but it has too many irritating errors to be of very much practical use.

Appendix C

Glossary

Burn   A brook or small stream.

Cess   A tax, usually a locally imposed one.

Drap   A drop or a small quantity of liquid.

Fauld dyke The stone wall surrounding a sheep-pen or fold.

Grange   A farm often associated with an abbey and sometimes well away from the immediate area of monastic buildings.

Haugh   Level ground by a river, water-meadow.

Heritable   Applied to immovable property (land and houses) which went by inheritance to a lawful heir.

Heritage   Property descending to an heir on the death of the owner.

Heritor   The proprietor of heritable property, a property-owner,

Heugh   A cliff or steep bank.

Kail (Kale) A type of curly cabbage, but often the term referred to a soup with kail as the main ingredient.

Laird   The landlord of landed property or an estate, often equated with the English squire.

March   Usually seen as 'The Marches', it denoted a boundary or frontier, from that of an entire country down to a field. Frequently used to describe sub-divisions of the Anglo-Scottish Border, which until the Union of the Crowns in 1603, was composed of three Marches on either side, all six under wardens whose impossible task was to keep the peace.

Merse   (With capital letter) The area of Berwickshire lying between the Lammermuir Hills and the Tweed, but often loosely used to refer to the whole county. Without a capital letter, it is used to describe the marshy lands adjoining the Solway Firth in Dumfriesshire.

NSA   New Statistical Account of Scotland - see Introduction.

OSA   Old Statistical Account of Scotland - see Introduction.

Policies   The enclosed grounds of a large house, the park of an estate.

Reivers   A term unique to the border country of both Scotland and England to describe the robbers, raiders, marauders and plunderers who terrorised the entire area until the 17th century, used especially when they went riding on a raid.

Roup   A sale or let by public auction.

Tacksman   A person who holds a lease, often used to refer to a turnpike toll keeper.

Water   A small river, in size between a burn and a river.

Index

(Coach names in *italics*)